MW01104262

Other Works by Del Marth and Martha J. Marth

The Florida Almanac® (annual edition)
The Florida Guide (annual edition)
The Rivers of Florida
Yesterday's Sarasota
The Florida Horse Owner's Field Guide
The Florida Dog Owner's Handbook
The Florida Cat Owner's Handbook

ST. PETERSBURG: ONCE UPON A TIME

ST. PETERSBURG:
ONCE UPON A TIME

Memories of Places & People 1890s to 1990s

DEL MARTH
MARTHA J. MARTH

Suwannee River Press

Way down upon the Suwannee...

ISBN: 1-885034-08-3

Suwannee River Press
9139 NW 9th Court
Branford FL 32008

TABLE OF CONTENTS

ACKNOWLEDGMENT

This edition of *St. Petersburg: Once Upon a Time* builds upon the original edition written by the authors in 1976. Expanding on that edition, the authors have updated text and photographs and thus have called upon numerous individuals who deserve a word of thanks.

Among them is the staff at the St. Petersburg Historical Museum, who diligently verified the existence of places and people, past and present. Former WSUN-TV personnel Bill Coletti and June Hurley Young provided leads and refreshed our memories. Linda Kinsey at the City Hall Information and Marketing Department proved a most helpful resource as did personnel at the City Parks Department. Longtime resident Eugene V. Marth personally double-checked city landmarks to verify their existence. And another longtime St. Petersburg resident, Earl F. "Skip" Campbell, perused photographs and summoned his recollections to help identify specific places and people.

All the efforts of these people helped produce a book that we hope will give young and old a memorable and entertaining view of St. Petersburg, which has always been — and remains — one of the nation's loveliest cities.

Photograph Credits:

Pages 174, 175, 177 photographs courtesy of the City of St. Petersburg.

Pages 72, 75, 78, 93, 95, 102, 103, 117, and the back cover, photographs courtesy of the Tampa-Hillsborough County Public Library System's Burgert Brothers Collection.

Pages 36, 37, 55, 56, 63, 79, 91, 113, 115, 116, 118, 137, 138, 139, 145, 146, 164, 167, photographs courtesy of the St. Petersburg Historical Museum.

Page 141, photograph courtesy of the Clearwater Public Library.

Other illustrations and photographs appeared in the 1976 edition of this work and were provided by the City News Bureau or were given to the authors by individual residents.

$\mathcal{L}$ike a child who puts his ear to the railroad track to hear the distant sounds of a faraway train, a time-traveler wishing to tune in on the past of St. Petersburg could choose no better site than to stand in the middle of Williams Park, close one's eyes, and hope to recapture the sounds of events there over the city's 10 decades of history.

For Williams Park is St. Petersburg's most enduring and symbolic landmark. Since 1888, when this four-acre oasis was deeded as a park, it has been the community's center, its heart. The speeches, the concerts, the celebrations taking place on its grounds, now as then, reveal more about St. Petersburg's way of life, its pursuit of happiness, than the bustle and play going on anywhere else within today's 58 square miles of city limits.

Williams Park in 1909.

The park's grounds during the passing century have been more hallowed and hailed than the city's famed beaches and wide streets. Felling one of its trees still prompts debate and controversy. Over the years, as St. Petersburg expanded outward and upward, with downtown real estate doubling in value time and again, proposals surfaced favoring the razing of old landmarks for new buildings, of leasing precious waterfront property to commercial enterprises, even of filling in the old city reservoir — Mirror Lake — for parking no less.

But no responsible citizen ever took leave of his senses to brazenly suggest Williams Park be sold off, that it would make a fancy site for a new office building or profitably accommodate a perpetual flea market.

Its presence has been preserved to honor the gentleman who literally put St. Petersburg on the map... and for whom the park is named — John C. Williams.

1

Bearded, autocratic Williams was a wealthy, but unhealthy, family man from Detroit. His affliction was asthma, for which his Michigan physician prescribed a warm climate. Determined to more fully enjoy life, and to lengthen his time on Earth if only for the sake of his wife and 10 dependent children, Williams in 1875 traveled up and down the Florida peninsula seeking an elixir. No particular spot suited him and he was preparing to return North to his family via boat from Cedar Key when he struck up a conversation with a stranger.

John C. Williams

Listening to Williams tell of his unsuccessful search, the stranger suggested the 58-year-old Michigan man delay his return one more week to explore a place known as Point Pinellas. A small peninsula dangling into two great bodies of water, Tampa Bay and the Gulf of Mexico, its remoteness from the usually traveled routes had left it relatively unknown and uninhabited.

Williams decided to take a look. Three days later, after a jolting wagon trip into the near virgin lands at the southern tip of Point Pinellas, he found his "Promised Land."

Basking in an average annual temperature of 71.6 degrees and nurtured by a pleasant 51 inches of rainfall yearly, Point Pinellas was not entirely unexplored or unsettled before the 19th Century. Indians camped on the peninsula for hundreds of years. But by the end of the 16th Century most tribes had abandoned their villages along Tampa Bay and Boca Ciega Bay to the ravages of Spanish explorers.

The native population left little to posterity, only the crude architecture of temple and burial mounds. But even this legacy was greater than that passed on by the Spaniards. Led by the temperamental Panfilo de Narvaez, the Spaniards put ashore on Point Pinellas in 1528, near what is now Park Street. Looking for gold and finding none, they stayed but two weeks, finally sailing their empty ships up the Gulf coast.

On his heels 11 years later came Panfilo's friend Hernando de Soto. More methodical but still singleminded, Hernando de Soto sought first to tame the Indians before robbing them of the gold he was certain sprinkled the lush land. He also cut a wider swath than his predecessor, scattering his nine ships along the peninsula shoreline from the mouth of Tampa Bay up inside to Safety Harbor. Frustrated by a fruitless search, he finally marched his men off into the interior to look elsewhere.

The pattern didn't change for decades. More conquistadores, led by long-forgotten explorers from the Old World, scoured the peninsula for gold and a "Fountain of Youth," moving on when the land failed to yield treasure and a potion for immortality.

The only accomplishment of the expeditions, if one chooses to view it as something positive, was the clearing of Indians from the peninsula to make future white settlement easier. The few Indians that did remain after the Spanish pillaging, or survived diseases brought by the explorers, either moved away or were carried off into slavery. Some became Seminoles, a loosely organized tribe made up primarily of Indians fleeing from the North.

Three hundred years were to pass from the time of the Spaniards' first probe in the area to the peninsula's first permanent white settler. The pioneer was Count Odet Philippe.

A former surgeon general of the French Navy, the Count's military career ended with his Navy's defeat in the Battle of Trafalgar. He had been taken prisoner and languished for two years in a Bahamian jail. Released in 1807, and after sojourns in South Carolina and near Florida's Indian River, the Count permanently established a plantation in 1823 along the bluffs of Safety Harbor. There he died in 1869. Philippe Park still honors the Frenchman and contains his remains. A greater recognition is his, however, for bringing orange and other citrus plants from the Caribbean to the Tampa Bay area.

At the southernmost end of the county another park bears the name of one of the Count's contemporaries. Antonio Maximo Hernandez established a fishery on the point of land now called Maximo in 1843. Among his neighbors was another fisherman, William Bunce, who settled down in the Mullet Key chain. Both were blown out of business by a storm historians reflect must have been the worst ever to strike the peninsula.

Known as "The Gale" of 1848, it bowled over the peninsula upending and inundating the entire Tampa Bay area, including the nearby village of Tampa with its 100 residents.

Exacting the toll was not the wind, estimated at a mere 70 miles per hour, but the tide. The waters rose and fell 15 feet within six hours. No lives were reported lost, but the land took an awesome beating. Islands were swept aside, old passes filled with sand and new ones scoured out (Johns Pass, among them).

"The bays met" was the way one oldtimer put it. For generations thereafter, "The Gale" became the measuring stick to calculate passage of time on the peninsula.

Aberrant behavior of nature etches indelible fears in man so, not surprisingly, it took nearly a decade before settlers wandered back. Abel Miranda led the return, setting up a fishery at Maximo; two years later, in 1859, the brothers William and John Bethell joined him. Their's was a short-lived enterprise, however, ended by the Civil War. In fact, nearly all life in the area disappeared when the fight started. Of course, only five families lived on Point Pinellas in 1861, but as soon as the conflict spread a little exodus began. Only one dwelling remained lighted.

"The Gale," then the Civil War — the peninsula must indeed have seemed bleak and without future in the 1860s. Roads were sand trails winding around forests. Streams had to be forged, there being no bridges. Building supplies and tools couldn't be purchased anywhere, even in the scraggy village of Tampa; if they were, the trip to Tampa had to be made on foot, or by ox cart, taking several days each way.

Inaccessibility, it seemed, was the peninsula's worst liability. Yet at the same time, this remoteness, this geographical seclusion, was also its chief asset. Being nearly surrounded by water, Point Pinellas basked in a perpetual sun while being fanned on three sides with offshore breezes. A natural thermostat controlled its climate, assuring pleasant Summers and mild Winters.

This was the peninsula as Williams saw it in 1875. So his difficult trek south with family members four years later — the last month by covered wagon from Gainesville — only made the goal more enticing.

He had, upon his discovery of Point Pinellas, purchased huge parcels of acreage on the peninsula so that when the Williamses arrived to establish their new home, it was to a 1,600-acre spread in what is now downtown St. Petersburg.

Once settled in, Williams made another discovery about Point Pinellas. The land promised more than it gave. He tried farming and failed miserably. The sandy soil would not take to his northern farming methods. For two years he persisted, then gave up. Hiring several men to oversee the land, Williams took his family back north. He needed some time to think about his next move.

Hardly had he finished unpacking when a story in the Detroit paper grabbed his attention. The dispatch reported that a wealthy Philadelphian named Hamilton Disston had recently purchased 4-million acres of Florida's publicly-owned land for $1-million. The transaction, Williams learned, made Disston owner of 110,000 acres in the peninsula area, more than 30,000 of them on Point Pinellas. (In fact, of the 37,000 acres now making up St. Petersburg, Disston bought 26,000 plus nearly all of what is now Gulfport.)

Disston had two traits that served him well — he thought big and he acted quickly. By 1884, three years after his purchase, the Philadelphian had formed the Disston City Land Co. and filed a plat of "Disston City." Spread over 12,000 acres, the city plat took in nearly all the southern end of the peninsula. Only two tracts were excluded — a portion of Big Bayou, and Williams's land.

Hamilton Disston

Before the year was out — on Christmas Eve, to be exact — enough folks populated Disston City to warrant a holiday celebration. A party was held in the 26-room Waldorf Hotel, just opened. By this time his city also had a wharf, a warehouse, and three store buildings, all along the present Gulfport waterfront.

Pouring thousands of dollars into promotion, Disston advertised heavily in the Northern newspapers. Disston City soon began attracting investors, as well as residents. The steamer *"Mary Disston"* started making regular trips from Tampa and Cedar Key to the sprouting village, disembarking newcomers in search of their mailorder plots. In less than a year, the Point's first newspaper — the *Sea Breeze* — was to begin reporting all the goings-on:

"Fine watermelons are being brought into town by our farmers"... "people are busy setting out sweet potato vines"... and an editorial pointed out "Disston City needs a good bathhouse, more interest in Sunday School, more frequent mails."

When the mail did arrive, it was addressed to the town of "Bonifacio." Postal officials refused to designate the post office as "Disston City" because of a town north of Tampa with the similar name of "Diston." The moniker "Bonifacio," the story goes, was the middle name of a Disston aide.

By 1885, Disston City, or "Bonifacio," appeared on its way to becoming a full-fledged city. What happened next must have buoyed still more the plans of Disston and his company.

A report came out of New Orleans that year from the 36th annual meeting of the American Medical Society. Convention delegates had gathered to hear, among other things, the results of a committee investigation led by a Dr. W. C. Van Bibber. The committee had been searching for the ideal location of a "Health City."

Such searches began following Civil War, when many citizens complained of "neurasthenia," a nervous condition. Some physicians linked the ailment to caffeine and tobacco. Other doctors blamed industrialization and urged their patients to relocate to healthier climes.

Dr. Van Bibber read his report:

PINELLAS PENINSULA

FOR RELIEF FROM

Consumption, Chronic Bronchitis, Rheumatism, Gout, Neurasthenia, AND KINDRED DISEASES.

"Where should such a Health City be built? Overlooking the deep Gulf of Mexico, with the broad waters of a beautiful bay nearly surrounding it; with but little now upon its soil but the primal forests, there is a large sub-peninsula, Point Pinellas, waiting the hand of improvement.

"Its average Winter temperature is 72 degrees; that its climate is peculiar, its natural products show; that its air is healthy, the ruddy appearance of its few inhabitants attest. Those who have carefully surveyed the entire state, and have personally investigated this sub-peninsula and its surroundings, think that it offers the best climate in Florida."

The report by Dr. Van Bibber was distributed widely. Perhaps nowhere was it read more thoroughly and more often than in Detroit, by Williams. He started to pack again, this time vowing to leave Michigan for good and return to his Florida acreage.

But he altered his plans a bit. He would not farm. He would build a city.

It was 1886. Williams built a home for his family in the now famous Hyde Park section of Tampa and then delved into ways of creating a town from his 1,600 acres on Point Pinellas. The first requirement was the most obvious, and the most challenging. Access. A means of easy access to the Point was critical.

Some historians contend Williams backed into the solution — a railroad. It is recorded, to be sure, that Hamilton Disston's company had first crack at getting the narrow gauge Orange Belt Railroad into Point Pinellas. The newly formed Orange Belt was laying tracks all over central Florida and its owner, a Russian immigrant, was eager to put down a spur to Point Pinellas.

But Disston and his aides made a disastrous decision. They rejected the terms offered by the railroad's owner.

The Russian, a hustling promoter who reveled in the free enterprise system, was Peter A. Demens. He wanted to put the terminus of the Orange Belt at Mullet Key, on deep water.

Disston offered Demens 25 percent of all the land he and all his companies owned within six miles of the rails if the railroad ended at Disston City. Disston was not about to finance the high costs of causeways and bridges out to Mullet Key, he informed Demens.

When the Russian persisted, Disston cut off the negotiations. And, one might add, also cut off any future for Disston City, too. In fact, within two years the town went into a permanent decline.

If Disston's dreams were stunted by the impasse with Demens, then it's likewise true that as a result of the impasse, Williams's visions approached fulfillment. For it took only two short months before Demens and Williams sought out each other, discussed terms, and contracted for the railroad to come to the Point via Williams's property. The terminus had changed, however; it was not to be Mullet Key, but Tampa Bay near what is now Central Avenue.

Peter Demens

Williams deeded 500 acres to the railroad in exchange for Demens' promise to lay the rails right through "town" to the waterfront, and then build a wharf out to where the water was 12 feet deep. That turned out to be a half-mile off shore.

Both men kept their part of the bargain though neither benefited greatly. Steamers and sailing vessels from Tampa did dock at the railroad pier, each exchanging passengers, but the railroad, with its uncomfortable narrow gauge ride, failed to entice large numbers of tourists. In fact, not until it was converted into standard gauge some seven years later did its reputation for dependability and service begin attracting tourists. The gauge change-over came when the railroad was leased (and eventually purchased) by wealthy Henry B. Plant of Tampa.

Nevertheless, the railroad did provide the impetus for the little village. When the first train puffed into town in 1888 only 30 people made up the populace. But expectations were great so a hotel was built — the Detroit. Cooled by overhead fans and heated by a fireplace, the 40-room structure at Central and Second Street was named after Williams's hometown. It was the only "major" building in the waterfront area other than an ornate depot put up on First Avenue South between Second and Third Streets.

Williams and Demens went ahead with a plat of the town, even though most of the residents seemed to cluster around Ninth Street rather than near the "downtown" the two men were trying to develop. But it wasn't long before Ninth Street merchants moved their shops. Seeing the railroad pier completed, the hotel finished, the steamers unloading passengers, they began relocating nearer the "future" of the village.

Filing a plat didn't require many specifications. The 1888 records show it covered just two square miles. The most detailed section was the waterfront. It was divided into 12 lots — each a sand flat or shoal. But rather than secure the waterfront against tides and erosion, a more important civic improvement needed attention. Central Avenue was barely passable for horse-drawn carts, virtually impassable for pedestrians. The Woman's Town Improvement Association built a wooden sidewalk.

As the "Gay Nineties" arrived, the Federal census counted 273 noses in the village, enough to prompt the outspoken to suggest it was time to incorporate. Citizens divided into the "wets" and the "drys" and in 1892 the village board took the vote.

The town's founder, Williams, lined up on the side of the "wets" and ran for mayor. He didn't have the majority with him, however, and though incorporation was voted in 15-11, Williams lost his race. Rejected, and not fully recovered from a stroke, he died two months later.

So as the Town of St. Petersburg approached the 20th Century, uncertain of its direction and future, its two major figures, men who "created" it, were gone. Demens had lost his railroad and moved on to California, leaving behind one significant legacy — the name of St. Petersburg. The story goes he and Williams drew straws over who would name the town, the loser getting to name the first hotel. Hometowns won in both instances — St. Petersburg (Russia) and Detroit (Michigan). One of the first acts of the Town Council, subscribers to a strong moral code that had no use for alcohol, was to build a jail. Measuring 10 x 12 feet, it cost $37.68.

As more money was raised from taxes and bond issues, town improvements became more noticeable. The first school was built, and wooden sidewalks along Central were replaced with shell, as were several roads. "The Swale," a quagmire at Central and Second Street that thwarted traffic, was filled in. A bank was needed, so one was organized. Williams Park, no more than a raw piece of land since it was deeded in 1888, was cleared and fenced to keep the cows out on "Park Day" in 1893. The first bandstand came two years later, a fixture the park has never been without. Seeing the new town take shape, the *West Hillsborough Times* moved down from Clearwater in 1892 (and grew into today's *St. Petersburg Times*).

Not a rich little town (its total valuation when incorporated was $123,000), St. Petersburg survived the 1894-95 "Big Freeze" with nary a sniffle nor a lost dollar. Other parts of Florida weren't as fortunate, so some citrus growers elsewhere, determined not to lose their crop again, relocated on temperate Point Pinellas. The population shot up to more than 1,000.

Railroad and recreation pier in 1890.

It was a step forward, but the town was soon back-pedaling. A second storm, this one from the sea, washed out the railroad pier. Plant, now controlling the railroad, decided not to rebuild. It was a decision, perhaps deliberately conceived, to prevent St. Petersburg from ever becoming a major port in competition with Tampa.

A year later, in 1896, another pier was constructed but its biggest use was recreation. Known as Brantley's Pier, it featured a bathing pavilion and a toboggan slide, both attracting more people than the structure's horse-drawn flat car meant to carry passengers and freight from ships to shore.

As the century neared an end, few results of Dr. Van Bibber's report to his medical colleagues about "The Health City" manifested themselves. One that did was the arrival of F. A. Davis. A Philadelphian, Davis read about the paradise of Point

Pinellas and moved, not to the southern tip but to Tarpon Springs. There he set up an electric plant, expecting it would generate enthusiasm among the citizens. It didn't, so Davis moved his 50-watt power station to St. Petersburg.

Nailing it together on the waterfront (site of the present day Yacht Club), Davis threw the switch in 1897, lighting up the little town — but from "sundown to midnight only."

To shopkeeper Arthur Norwood, the electricity was less needed than a telephone. With one store on Ninth Street and another "downtown," he suffered from lack of communication. So he hooked up his own phone system — two phones, one in each store. By the next year, 1899, St. Petersburg boasted 18 subscribers dialing each other via a new public phone system.

Squeezing in still another utility that year, the town sold $10,000 in bonds to build a water tank near Reservoir Lake (Mirror Lake).

And so the 1800s ended.

The Town of St. Petersburg was, it thought, ready for the 20th Century. Its population New Year's Eve was 1,575. That didn't count the tourists coming in and out of town, of course, nor was anyone very much aware just how significant the presence of those tourists would become.

One, in fact, a 30-year-old Kentucky pharmacist who came to town for the first time in the Winter months of 1899 on his wedding trip, was to become a prime architects of the town's future.

He was C. Perry Snell.

If the last decade could be characterized as a period in which the Town of St. Petersburg was seeking a direction, the opening decade of the 1900s was a time of preparation, of getting things in order. For it was obvious St. Petersburg had a future; what wasn't clear was what kind of a future.

Some pointed toward the railroad, contending the peninsula town might make a great rail terminal for shipping.

Then there was the water, on all three sides. Wouldn't it make sense to work toward become a major port?

Not so clearly defined, but certainly to be considered, was St. Petersburg as a resort. Wasn't its climate ideal, its location unsurpassed?

All these, and more, were on the minds of the town's leaders when the new century entered. But despite their different visions, all were aware their goal in the years ahead was to improve and refine life on the peninsula.

One of the first orders of business was broadening its government. Thus, in 1903, St. Petersburg officially took on the status of a City. Meetings were held in a new City Hall on First Avenue South next to the old jail. A new jail, in the same block, was headquarters for a five-man police force, which included the $100-a-month police chief.

The city's first bank went under in 1902 when it got involved in an unsuccessful phosphate company. Lost were $51,000 in deposits. But another, the West Coast Bank, started up in 1903.

More modern and inclusive phone connections were needed. F. A. Davis took care of that. He bought out the existing system, then promptly sold it all to the Brorein Company of Tampa, a part of the Peninsular Telephone Company (which later sold to General Telephone).

For entertainment, a new medium was brought into town. They were motion pictures, now showing at the new Royal Palm Theatre next to the Detroit Hotel.

Meanwhile, the Chamber of Commerce was determined to fill the new city with free-spending tourists. It ordered up 10,000 promotional booklets. The copy talked about the unexcelled fishing, the healing properties of waves of salt water, the constant sunshine, even the vast choice of accommodations. And a choice there was. City hotels offered more than 675 rooms in 1905. There was the Detroit, the Manhattan, the Colonial, the Huntington, the Wayne, the Chautauqua, the Paxton, and the Belmont.

Of course, no sizeable group of people can live together without forming a club. So when newcomers learned many of their neighbors came originally from Illinois, the obvious result was the Illinois Tourist Society. It was the first of a string of tourist societies for which St. Petersburg became famous.

Just how tourists and new residents made it to the new city in the early 1900s took some enterprise. Automobiles were a rarity. When the first one drove into St. Petersburg in 1905 — an "Orient" purchased by E. H. Tomlinson — folks ran out of the shops to view the commotion. The next year another car, muddied and loaded down with baggage, motored into town from — it was hard to believe — Detroit, Michigan. The first tourist had arrived by car. It took him 14 days.

As for driving to nearby Tampa in those days, the trip still was long and arduous. In 1907 a party of motorists left Tampa for St. Petersburg, for example. Zig-zagging around swamps and swales, the wheels often sinking hub deep in mud or sand, the party needed three and a half days "on the road" to make the trip.

It was far easier to cross the bay between the two cities by steamer. An "Independent Line" with two steamers had been operating since 1899, when in 1906 F. A. Davis formed the Tampa Bay Transportation Co. Tearing down Brantley's Pier, Davis built a larger one, the Electric Pier. It extended 3,000 feet out into the bay to unload passengers from his 500-passenger *Favorite*." Fairly successful, Davis soon had competition from other maverick steamer lines, all fighting for a dominant role in freight and passenger commerce they felt sure was to come to St. Petersburg via the water.

The railroad had other ideas. Still struggling with its corporate structure, the original Orange Belt line, after widening its track, changed its name to the Sanford & St. Petersburg Railway, then, in 1902, became a part of the great Atlantic Coast Line. It was not about to default on the waterfront trade, but in Davis it had come up against one of the city's most innovative businessmen. For hardly had Davis finished his "Electric Pier" out into the bay when the reason for the nickname became clear. He planned a trolley line, right out into the water. Having gotten a franchise for a street car line in 1902, Davis spent nearly three years raising capital from his wealthy friends in Philadelphia. By 1905 he had trolleys running from Ninth Street to the waterfront; a year later the line expanded to Tangerine Avenue, then west to 55th Street and south to Boca Ciega Bay.

Except for a Sunday afternoon ride, few passengers made the run that far west. But then Davis and his backers were gambling their street cars would promote real estate development in that area. One location being pushed that year was the defunct Disston City. It was renamed Veteran City in 1905. The new name and promotion was aimed at Civil War veterans, beseeching them to live out their days on beautiful Boca Ciega Bay.

But the Davis gamble failed and his "empire" tumbled. In 1907 his land company, boat lines, trolley company, power plant — all were thrown into receivership.

Davis wasn't the only one having his problems trying to promote and develop St. Petersburg. Proponents of a city-owned waterfront also were fighting for survival of their idea.

In 1902, the waterfront was in an unsightly condition. Citizens sought government aid but because the property was privately owned, no funds were allocated. So another tack was taken. In 1905 a group of waterfront boosters, the Board of Trade, decided to buy several key waterfront properties and hold them until the City Council could purchase them. The maneuver succeeded. Not only did the Council quickly buy the parcels, it took options on adjacent waterfront land. The invaluable property extended roughly from Fifth Avenue North (then the city limits) to the basin now known as Bayboro Harbor. Only two parcels in the expanse remained privately owned — the one held by the electric company and the other by the ACL railroad.

It has never been a point of argument just who was primarily responsible for preserving St. Petersburg's most precious asset — its waterfront. W. L. Straub, owner and editor of the *Times*, fought continuously, in his private hours and on the editorial page, for public ownership.

The second-guessers may suggest Straub's competitor — Maj. Lew Brown, owner and editor of the *Independent* at the time — made an equally significant contribution to the future of his city. Brown's brainchild was the famous "Sunshine Offer," a free newspaper any day the sun did not shine on St. Petersburg. It became known the world over.

Also as famous (or infamous, depending on your viewpoint) for its effect on St. Petersburg was still another promotion springing up about the same time. Credited is Noel Mitchell, a real estate salesman with the interest of his customers uppermost.

In 1908 Mitchell opened an office at Fourth and Central. It was at the time sort of a halfway location between the waterfront and the populous Ninth Street area. When customers dropped in, he noticed they were tired from the walk, so he ordered some benches — 50 of them.

Painting them orange and printing on their backs "Mitchell the Sand Man" — "The Honest Real Estate Dealer" — "He Never Sleeps," the thoughtful salesman set them out on the sidewalk in front of his office.

The results came quickly. Everybody was congregating in front of Mitchell's office. Soon other merchants bought benches to place in front of their shops. In no time, Central Avenue was lined with benches.

Unfortunately they were not uniform in color or size so the thoroughfare took on the flavor of a midway. The mayor solved that problem in one stroke — he sponsored an ordinance requiring the bench size be standardized and all of them painted the same color — green.

When the decade ended, St. Petersburg still was primping for its debut, whatever form it took The city now, in 1910, was home to 4,127. And, unknown to most of them, the first "boom" was on its way.

Subtle hints cropped up. Charles Roser, the "Fig Newton" creator, for example, bought 30 acres along Booker Creek, and talked about building an elegant neighborhood of fine homes. George S. Gandy, a friend of Philadelphians Disston and Davis, purchased the corner of Central and Fifth Street to build what many folks thought certainly would be a "white elephant": — the La Plaza Theatre. Instead, it blossomed into one of the city's most popular and unique attractions. Meanwhile, C. Perry Snell, the Kentuckian who had been wintering in Florida, built a home in St. Petersburg and invested heavily in lots and acreage, particularly to the north of the city. With J. C. Hamlett, in 1911 he launched the North Shore development.

Private enterprise was hustling. But so was government. Working since 1908 to separate from the county government of Hillsborough, officials and politicians finally succeeded in 1911. St. Petersburg now was in a new, and its own, county — Pinellas. Naturally, it made plans to be the county seat, but an aggressive and versatile group of politicians to the north, in Clearwater, spliced together a courthouse overnight, and there it stayed.

Stung but undaunted, St. Petersburg's leaders pushed on. Expanding its city limits for the first time since its incorporation, the city moved its southern boundaries to 17th Avenue South. By 1914, it had expanded twice more, north to 22nd Avenue, and west to Boca Ciega Bay. With its westward thrust, the city opened Central Avenue all the way to the bay and ran the trolley lines down its middle.

Deciding it preferred brick roads to marl, after an experiment that showed marl failed to hold up, the Council voted to brick more than 75 miles in the city limits. It put up a gas plant, bought the trolley company for $175,000, built the Open-air post office, erected a public library with help from Andrew Carnegie, and got approval from the U.S. Government for a harbor at Bayboro.

The Bayboro decision once and for all sealed St. Petersburg's waterfront for parks and the people. For when applying for Federal funds for Bayboro, the city vowed to remove all water commerce from its piers and property near the foot of Central Avenue, channeling any shipping, instead, into the Bayboro Harbor.

The agreement prompted building of the first Municipal Pier, a wooden structure, complemented in 1913 on North Mole by a modern bathhouse, solarium, and beach — The Spa. To further improve the waterfront appearance, the old "Electric Pier" was demolished.

Medical facilities got prompt attention, too. The city already had a hospital — the Samaritan Emergency Hospital built in 1910. But it was no more than a cottage, soon inadequate for the growing population. With private contributions and a bond issue, the city built Augusta Memorial Hospital, named after the mother of a benefactor, E. H. Tomlinson. (Built on the site of the present Bayfront Medical Center, its name was later changed to City Hospital, then Mound Park Hospital.)

Fortunately for the city, one of its leading citizens at the time also was a fanatic follower of major league baseball teams. Al Lang, who went on to become the city's first mayor in 1916 under its new charter, wanted a ball team training in St. Petersburg. With his enthusiasm and connections in the sport, he got one, in 1914, the St. Louis Browns. And a year later, the Philadelphia Phillies were hitting fungos in the "Sunshine City."

Lang never stopped pitching; he brought an Indianapolis team in for training in 1921, the Boston Braves from 1922 to 1937, the New York Yankees from 1925 to 1961. Now headquartered in St. Petersburg during the Spring, the St. Louis Cardinals have been here since 1938, the New York Mets since 1962. Thanks to St. Petersburg's own big leaguer, Al Lang, residents and tourists have enjoyed Major League baseball continuously since 1922.

Al Lang

By this time, it was obvious the direction St. Petersburg was heading. It had opted to be a resort city, a mecca for tourists.

The barrage of Chamber of Commerce ads in northern cities unquestionably had an impact. In January 1913, for example, the first special train just for tourists — 200 of them from Ohio and Indiana — pulled into the depot. Spotting the trend, the Detroit Hotel quickly added 60 rooms, and expanded its dining room to serve 300.

Certain that more Yankees would be fleeing the cold North, a second railroad started up — the Tampa & Gulf Coast Railroad. Its prediction was right. In 1914 its first passenger train pulled in — 15 coaches packed with 1,500 visitors (larded heavily, it was suspected, with excursionists from up county and Tampa). The second railroad flourished for many decades but under a different name; only a year after the Tampa line started up it was absorbed by the Seaboard Air Line.

Still another mode of transportation invaded the city in 1914. The first commercial airboat line in the nation revved up on St. Petersburg's waterfront. Twice daily folks in a hurry could fly to Tampa. Elapsed time: 18 minutes.

The excitement of what was happening to St. Petersburg was contagious. People came into it by rail by car, by boat. Roads were being paved, utility companies started, schools and hospitals and theatres constructed, hotel and dining rooms expanded, bathhouses and baseball diamonds built.

Cognizant of it all were men such as H. Walter Fuller, C. Perry Snell, C. A. Harvey, all savvy in the art of buying land, subdividing it, and selling it lot by lot.

Starting in 1911, Fuller raised enough money, again from the Philadelphia crowd, to draft a grandiose plan. He envisioned populating St. Petersburg all the way from 16th Street to Boca Ciega Bay, a half-mile each side of Central Avenue. Buying up land at $5 or less per acre, and bargaining with the city over road paving, he soon had laid out the largest area of the city ever planned as one residential site. One of the first improvements was construction of the St. Petersburg Country Club (later to become the Jungle Golf Course), opened New Year's Day 1916.

Meanwhile, Snell was buying and developing St. Petersburg northward along the shores of Tampa Bay. His goal was to establish North Shore as the premier address in town. Shrewd yet sensitive, Snell eventually owned nearly all of the city north of Fifth Avenue North and east of Fourth Street.

Working on a less grand scale, Harvey sought his profit in the large tract of swampy acreage at the mouths of Salt Creek and Booker Creek. He was an enthusiastic booster of Bayboro Harbor, dedicated to creating a commercial port in the undeveloped basin. When Federal approval came, the dredging of the harbor created valuable residential property to the south. A real estate salesman, Harvey enticed Winter visitors to the property and no doubt sold enough to consider buying up more raw land still farther south of the city. But a heart attack killed him in 1914.

All three developers plus a battery of salesmen engaged in a lot-selling spree from 1911 to 1914. More than 20,000 residential lots had been created. Not all of them sold, but the action got so heavy at times that lots often got resold, and resold again, by the buyers, each successive owner looking to make a profit.

Fuller pinpointed the end of the little "boom" as the Summer of 1914, when the assassination in Europe set off the beginning of World War I. Whatever ended it, the "boom's" early effects still exist. City limits were greatly expanded. Along with the spread, an overall street system was devised, considered still to be one of the most simple and understandable in use. Thoroughfares were planned, then built, partially accounting for wide streets and roadways with boulevards between them.

Negative effects evolved, too. The obvious one was scattered lots, thousands of them, around the city, with only a house here and there. Less obvious was the financial loss incurred by many people, including developers that became engulfed in the flurry of land speculation. But it was a lesson that didn't take. In 10 years it would happen all over again.

Coming of World War I and this country's entry in 1917 stifled growth and people's plans. For the first time in nearly a generation, the future was impossible to perceive.

The psychological letdown resulted from fewer tourists, from tighter money, from the news now and then that a local boy had died in action. The first such tragedy came in 1916 with news of the death of Tony Jannus, the young aviator known city-wide. He was killed in the Russian Aero Service.

Many young men in the county answered the first draft registration in 1917. Each month a handful would catch the train to some military camp. Meanwhile, the Coast Artillery in town was called en masse to report to Fort Dade.

Tony Jannus

Following a call by President Wilson, the Pinellas Home Guards were organized in August 1917, charged with affording protection to the county.

On the homefront, four Liberty Loan drives were conducted, each one oversubscribed.

When the armistice whistles blew on Nov. 11, 1918, and the city took stock of the war's effect on it, the greatest loss was its young men. Eighteen died in uniform.

The economic pause between 1914 and 1919 in St. Petersburg was not entirely devoid of progress. To the immediate north, F. A. Davis, still searching for a successful long-range venture, resurfaced with a plan to build a new town — Pinellas Park. But first he had to drain the area, starting up the Cross Bayou Drainage District. Farther west, the area acquired its first bridge, the Seminole Bridge crossing Long Bayou.

None of the natives showed any interest in Gulf beaches, what with its infestation of mosquitoes. Enough newcomers found it exciting though, so W. D. McAdoo in 1919 connected the offshore islands with the mainland. He built a wooden span from what is now 87th Avenue at St. Petersburg Beach to the shore near Fifth Avenue South. To pay for it, he slapped on a toll.

Building a bridge from the mainland to the beaches was good for the Gulf communities, but the span that was to mean the most to St. Petersburg was still on the drawing board. Ever since 1902, when George S. Gandy first visited St. Petersburg, he dreamed of a shortcut route between Tampa Bay's two "major cities." At the time, the shortest route around the edge of the bay was 43 miles. He believed he could cut the trip to 19 miles by building a bridge across old Tampa Bay.

Came 1915 and he was ready to begin the mammoth job. Hiring surveyors, he determined the shortest line running across the shallowest depths. Rights of way were bought up in both Pinellas and Hillsborough counties. But then the delays set in.

It took nine months to secure War Department approval to cross navigable waters. Then the Florida Legislature needed time to pass bills permitting construction across the bay.

Just when Gandy was ready to proceed, the war broke out. Construction materials became scarce. He waited till the war ended, then found out the cost of post-war materials was prohibitive.

So while Gandy reassessed and refinanced his aging dream, St. Petersburg timidly embarked into the 1920s.

Looking back to The Twenties, and the suddenness and the madness of that decade's Great Land Boom, the historian keeps searching for the flamboyant business deal, the banner headline that had to launch such a financial spectacular.

But nothing of the sort ever happened. Instead, the beginnings always trace back to two families, names unknown, who pitched a tent on city property at 18th Street South and Second Avenue. Even the date is recorded — Aug. 26, 1920.

With the war over, tourists began trickling back to the Sunshine City for vacations. Unnoticed was the lack of accommodations to handle the increasing numbers, so when the two families were discovered tenting, the Chamber of Commerce tried getting them into a hotel or rooming house. But the "No Vacancy" signs were everywhere. Finally, Mayor Noel Mitchell was called. Let them stay, he suggested, and the city would install some makeshift sanitary facilities.

Two days later there were 20 families on the grounds, then 50. In two weeks, homemade camper trucks, their tarpaulins making lean-tos, crowded in and "Tent City" boasted a population of 120 families.

First to realize the significance of "Tent City" were the hotel men and the land speculators. They went to work fast. It didn't matter to them where the migration was coming from, nor how the tourists were getting to St. Petersburg. To the real estate salesmen, the campers were ripe for a sales pitch.

But to the Chamber, the influx was a statistic requiring analysis, and their questionnaires told something about the advancing "boom." Nearly 80 percent of the tourists were driving to St. Petersburg, many in Henry Ford's Model Ts. Only a few years earlier, 80 percent of the city's visitors came by train. And the new breed wanted to stay in a hotel, not an apartment or rooming house as did their predecessors.

In addition, the 1920s crowds carried more money on them. Before the war, the bulk of the tourists sometimes toted their own groceries down from the North; the new breed wanted to eat in restaurants. No longer did the wisecrack apply that circulated years earlier, i.e., the St. Petersburg tourist arrived with one shirt and a $20 bill and never changed either all Winter.

The Twenties' tourist not only had more than a $20 bill; he was eager to spend and invest some of the money he left under the mattress at home up North.

Borrowing funds as fast as they could, hotel men started building. In five years, from 1920 to 1925, a dozen big hotels went up — the Soreno, the Pheil (later the Madison), the Ponce de Leon, the Suwannee, the Mason (now the Princess Martha), the Pennsylvania, the Dennis, the Vinoy Park, the Jungle Country Club (now Admiral

Farragut Academy), the Rolyat (now Stetson Law College), the Don Ce Sar, the Royal Palm (demolished in the 1960s).

The arrival of one of St. Petersburg's worst storms — the 1921 hurricane — failed to dampen the developing "boom" though it did raise havoc along the waterfront. Piers that extended into the bay were destroyed by 10-foot tides; a report that Pass-a-Grille had been wiped out, its residents all dead, proved to be false in every respect, but records indicate that the Gulf and Boca Ciega Bay met over the land area to a depth of three feet. Borrowing $10,000 from businessmen, the City of St. Petersburg rebuilt its Municipal Pier and got back to the "boom" business.

Aware that the city was old enough for a history, officials chartered and built a Historical Museum along the waterfront. Shuffleboard courts were marked out for tourists at Mirror Lake. And the trolley lines worked to capacity.

Meanwhile, Gandy finally got it all together. Starting in 1922, 1,500 workmen began constructing the long overwater highway. Costing $3 million, it was 24-feet wide, contained 3 1/4 miles of causeway, 2 1/2 miles of bridge, and took two years to finish.

On Nov. 24, 1924, more than 30,000 attended the dedication, among them 17 state governors. After a ceremonious ride across, motorists were required to stop at toll booths and pay 75 cents per car and driver, plus 10 cents for each passenger. (Later, the toll dropped to 65 cents plus 10 cents, then 35 cents flat, and finally in 1944, because of the war, the government ordered elimination of the tolls).

The bridge inaugurated an entire new era. What had plagued St. Petersburg since its founding — in accessibility — now virtually dissipated. Only opening of the southern tip of Point Pinellas to permit travel south remained undone. And for the moment, that problem was being partially solved by the Bee Line Ferry. Making eight trips daily, the rundown ferry boats shortened the distance between St. Petersburg and Bradenton by 46 miles. Started in 1926, the Bee Line carried cars and passengers, taking 45 minutes to make the crossing.

Gandy Bridge soon after opening.

Gandy Bridge didn't hamper the ferry business to the south but it did eliminate the steamer traffic across Tampa Bay to St. Petersburg's waterfront. The last steamer sailed off in 1924.

The newspaper edition carrying the headline "St. Petersburg, Tampa United" also carried full-page ads by real estate companies. They knew full well the impact Gandy Bridge would have on development of St. Petersburg's north side. It was noted, for example, that when Gandy first began his project, an acre north on Fourth Street could be bought for $50. The day the bridge opened some speculators asked $5,000 an acre, and got it.

But land sales and big prices were everywhere. Snell Isle prior to the 1920s "boom" was mostly under water. Only 39 of the island's 275 acres poked above the mangroves. But when Snell finished filling and subdividing, he sold lots totaling more than $7 million in a few days. Helping entice prospective buyers were two Mediterranean Revival buildings he constructed — the Snell Isle Garden Apartments and the Sunset Golf & Country Club.

On the west side, Jack Taylor scooped up 600 acres of wild land and 2,000 lots for a quarter-million dollars, then set about to create the Pasadena area. Thinking big and loose, he poured a fortune into the spectacularly beautiful Spanish-style Rolyat Hotel. On opening day in 1926 guests included baseball's Babe Ruth and golf's Walter Hagen.

To the north of Taylor's enterprise, Walter Fuller hustled lots in the Jungle section, swaying buyers with a new hotel, a golf course, and a 320-acre airfield.

Down at City Hall, officials and employees scrambled to keep up. The year 1923 pushed St. Petersburg to the "fastest building" city in Florida, based on permits issued. Tourism was up 40 percent over the previous year. Forms for real estate licenses couldn't be kept in stock; by 1925, 6,000 real estate salesmen were hawking building lots. Most of them were succeeding for that year the city issued $25 million in building permits.

Up and down the streets merchants and businessmen tried to keep pace. To entertain the tourists and the increasing permanent population, the $250,000 Coliseum opened its doors in 1924 to one of the South's finest dance floors. Soon to take the stage were Paul Whiteman, Louis Armstrong, Buddy Rich and all the Big Bands.

At the same time, Florida Power Corporation erected its headquarters downtown at First Avenue South and Fifth Street, a year before the Grand Opening of the 2,300-seat Florida Theatre across the street. Also across from the Florida Power headquarters an architectural treasure, the YMCA, opened its rooms and swimming pool.

Everyone it seemed was making money or preparing to, and none knew how better than Doc Webb. In 1925 he opened the city's first cut-rate drug store. By offering all merchandise at 10 percent less than it could be purchased elsewhere, Webb soon was running the "World's Most Unusual" and the biggest drug store in the country.

On paper, the "boom" blew up in late 1925. But the city kept right on growing and building, caught up in its own momentum.

Leaders called upon voters to expand the city limits another 38 square miles, and they did. Out in Tampa Bay the second-floor ballroom floor at the Million Dollar Pier got a final sanding in preparation for its official opening in 1926.

James Earl "Doc" Webb

At nearby Bayboro Harbor, U. S. Coast Base #21 was welcomed to St. Petersburg, the New York Yankees took to the Spring training field at Crescent Lake Field, and the Goodyear blimp regularly floated into the city's waterfront air park.

But to men like Fuller, the "boom" was over. In the beginning of 1925 he estimated his fortune at $7 million. At year's end he had lost it all.

As for Taylor and his dreams in the Pasadena area, by the end of 1925 he had simply turned his back on the entire nightmare and went back North.

Snell showed more staying power. Still trying to sell lots on Snell Isle at "boom's" end, he reportedly had more money in the bank when the bust arrived than anyone — some $3 million. He didn't stop building. His next project was the towering Snell Building at Fourth and Central, completed in 1929 at a cost of $750,000.

Nevertheless, the pace had truly slackened. Banks holding useless paper went under. The city itself was on shaky ground. Its bonded indebtedness between 1927 and 1930 figured out to $802.06 owed by every resident, the second highest per capita indebtedness in the country.

Though St. Petersburg's population nearly tripled during the decade, from 14,237 in 1920 to 40,425, the change of "bigger" was not "best" for the citizens.

Jobs soon became scarce, and so did money. A Citizen's Emergency Committee had to be formed to issue scrip to pay people lucky enough to have work.

Fortunately, everyone was unaware of a greater financial bust about to confront them.

"Black Thursday," the day of the stock market crash in October 1929, turned much of America topsy-turvy. St. Petersburg already was saturated with bad news in its own marketplace so the Wall Street failure appeared as more of a sequel than an interruption to its economy. The city's residents took little comfort in the fact the entire country was wallowing in an economic backwash yet they felt doubly struck by the tidal-wave Depression. In many cities, some normal annual construction continued but in St. Petersburg nothing needed building because the city "overbuilt" in the 1920s. Thus, St. Petersburg not only wilted from the national Depression but suffered still further from conditions it brought upon itself during the "boom."

For example, payment in scrip was a scourge to which few American cities had to resort. The county's School Board paid its teachers in scrip. At the *St. Petersburg Times*, employees received half their pay in dollars, the other half in paper coupons. They could use the scrip for groceries at any store that advertised in the newspaper. In turn, the advertisers paid their ad bills in scrip.

Thankfully, most folks and merchants had confidence that whoever issued the chits would redeem them for merchandise. Scrip came in small denominations, usually $1, $5, $10, and change, but $100 coupons were seen in circulation. A few enterprising citizens even made money out of the emergency measure, buying $1 in scrip for 90 cents cash.

As expected, prices everywhere hit rock bottom. But none reached the low level advertised by Doc Webb at his famous drug store.

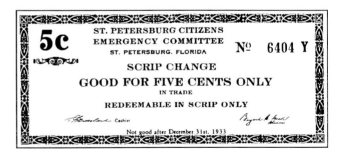

A promoter par excellence, Webb made national news with an astonishing three-cent breakfast. It included a small glass of orange juice, an egg, a strip of bacon, a piece of buttered toast, and a cup of coffee.

Thousands ate breakfast together every morning at the Webb's City counter. Everybody, it seemed, could dig up three cents. But not many accumulated enough money that year to pay their taxes. The City of St. Petersburg reported tax collections dropped 48 percent. Property was lost by scores of folks who couldn't meet their tax bills each year. For those few who still had a bankroll, and patience, it was a golden opportunity to become a land baron. Several did. They bought up thousands of lots and acres merely by paying the back taxes on them.

Twenty years later they were millionaires.

By 1933 the value of building permits in the city dropped to $381,650. Only eight years before they had reached $25 million. But efforts were made by a few businessmen to get something started, to stem the economic free-fall. Anything, even a movie studio.

On Weedon Island, for example, the Sun Haven Studios went into production. Buster Keaton came to town to star in the films. Three were made, every one a disaster. Despite continuing dreams of being a movie-making capital, St. Petersburg never got back into the film business after the Weedon Island fiasco.

One series of projects did take hold in St. Petersburg during the Depression. It wasn't a local effort, however, but one created in Washington D.C. The projects were the Works Progress Administration (WPA) and the Public Works Administration (PWA) and other work-finding legislation rushed through Congress by President Roosevelt. Men were hired to clean streets and ditches, to clear land for parks. Bartlett Park was one of those built during the New Deal. Under the PWA St. Petersburg also got itself a new City Hall. Bay Pines, a $1-million hospital built on an 800-acre spread in the sparsely settled west end of town, was another Depression baby.

Nearby, the Rolyat Hotel was seeking a new tenant. It finally sold to the Florida Military Academy.

A significant day in aviation occurred on Oct. 1, 1934, when a four-passenger plane took off from the downtown airfield named after Albert Whitted. (He had run a flying service there before a fatal plane crash in 1923.) The passenger plane headed for Daytona Beach, marking the beginning of National Airlines.

Overall, however, it was a depressing decade, to the pocket and to the stomach. But life in St. Petersburg during the 1930s was not a total bore or chore. With time on their hands, the city's oldsters organized the famous Kids and Kubs softball teams. Downtown theaters filled the house every "Bank Nite," when prizes were given away between the featured films. Even the Gulf beaches beckoned an increasing number of city folks, their day-to-day problems vanishing in the lull of the warm surf.

So St. Petersburg dragged itself into 1940. Again, the population had increased over the decade, from 40,425 to 60,812. It was the smallest gain, percentage-wise, since the city's founding. But it also was a sign that St. Petersburg's future had not passed, that it was still ahead.

The City of St. Petersburg was great war duty.

Shortly after Pearl Harbor, thousands of young men began training at waterfront park. They were quartered in fancy hotels once occupied by affluent tourists, swam in the Gulf of Mexico, tanned under the palm trees. They wrote home to Mother not to worry about them, that they were being fed all right and were stationed in one of the most beautiful places they had ever seen.

The Army was wise to choose the city for a training site. St. Petersburg's climate was mild and stable, and the city offered abundant hotel rooms. The city was a natural, not just for the Army and its Air Corps but for the other services as well.

Out at Pinellas County Airport on old Tampa Bay, the U.S. Government hurried along its construction (started in 1941) and used it as a training base for fighter pilots. To its original 710 acres it added an adjacent 600 acres, and constructed barracks for 1,500 men.

By Spring 1942, roll call for the Army Air Corps trainees in St. Petersburg was answered by 10,000 men. The number had doubled by Fall.

At Bayboro Harbor the Merchant Marine was training its volunteers, while nearby the U.S. Coast Guard beefed up its services, constantly patrolling the bay and the Gulf for enemy ships.

Brimming in khaki, the city marched off in an emotional high. To residents it was a dizzying about-face from events less than a year earlier. Still fresh in their vision were empty hotels, restaurants without diners, beaches sans bathers. Now, hotels overflowed, bar owners ordered more stools. Out on the beaches, every ray of sun was soaked up by a white-skinned recruit. Street traffic snarled trying to avoid marching platoons. And day and night Jeeps and military vehicles coursed up and down the peninsula.

Of the city's dozens of hotels, only the Suwannee at First Avenue North and Fifth Street was devoid of soldiers (it was agreed the hotel would remain available for commercial guests.) Even so, the constant influx of more soldiers necessitated putting up a "Tent City" in the Jungle area. Some 15,000 were housed there.

Each wave of recruits stayed but four to six weeks, learning the basics of soldiering. When transferred, their replacements moved in. Estimates of the number of miliary personnel in St. Petersburg during the war reached 120,000.

The figure did not include the thousands at MacDill Field in Tampa, many of whom used their weekend pass to come to St. Petersburg and the Gulf beaches. The MacDill migration increased still more dramatically when in 1944 President Roosevelt removed the toll from Gandy Bridge.

St. Petersburg over the years had become used to sudden and sizeable influxes of people with the result that residents took the new flurry of activity in stride. Even the wartime restrictions got respectful compliance. Nights were blacked out, car headlights got a coat of dark paint, gasoline rationing tightened (an "A" sticker was good for five gallons a week), and the maximum speed was set at 35 mph. Clutching green ration books, housewives judiciously doled out stamps for portions of scarce meats, butter, and sugar.

St. Petersburg Air Corps, 1941.

Near the war's end in 1945, with most of the soldiers departed from St. Petersburg for overseas posts, the city's population showed a 25,000 increase. A study attributed the jump to rejuvenated tourism. The newcomers were getting good news from both battlefronts, Europe and the Pacific, indicating the war was winding down.

On V-J Day, in August 1945, St. Petersburg found itself nearly as full of people as during the early war years.

Its residents' hopes and spirits and optimism also came alive. They again began to rebuild.

Long-range plans for civic improvements were drafted, and with new revenue from a bond funding program, projects began. New streets, fire stations, a new police station, and a hospital were built. The street car line, a fixture in St. Petersburg since near the turn of the Century, was replaced with buses.

Still a baseball town, the city now boasted Spring training sites for two Major League teams. In appreciation, and for the comfort of the thousands of tourists coming down for the March and April games, the city built Al Lang Field on the waterfront. It was dedicated in 1947.

A cloud remained over the housing situation. Both the city and Pinellas County books contained thousands of parcels on which taxes remained delinquent. Finally, the Legislature gave approval to a bill that allowed the governments to seize title to them. The effect was not instant but, like a slowly unfolding drama, its impact in the late 1940s drew crowds to the steps of the Courthouse and City Hall.

Under the law, the city was free to auction off seized lots. At first, attendance was sparse. But as the word got around, a frenzy of bidders showed up. Prices were what might be considered absurd today. Lots in choice sections of the city, including Snell Isle, sometimes sold for $10 or $20. A local attorney bought some 200 lots in Fuller's Jungle area for about $50 apiece, lots that Fuller had sold back in the 1925 "boom" for as much as $2,000 each.

Not everyone attending the auctions was a real estate agent or a land speculator. Many turned out to be former servicemen, ex-soldiers who had been stationed in St. Petersburg during the war and who came back to build a life here.

In "appreciation" for their service, the city one day held an auction solely for veterans. But the rules were changed. Each veteran drew a number. The price of each lot was nominal. Holder of the number drawn got the first choice of all the lots being auctioned.

To the benefit of St. Petersburg, the newcomers that were discovering the Sunshine City in the early 1950s, or returning to it after war duty here, didn't buy lots for reselling at a profit. They came and bought to build not only a home but a career and a life on the peninsula.

As a result, the economic and social changes that were about to occur were more permanent and lasting than those of the flamboyant and noisy land "boom" of the 1920s. This 1950s boom, an historian reflected, was a human invasion, a revolution in living, compared to the 1925 "poker game with vacant lots for chips."

The incoming housing tide of the 1950s also brought with it innovations in development and construction. In the 1920s, a speculator cleared his recently bought acreage, filed a plat, maybe put down a road or two, and began selling. Not so in the 1950s.

Buyers of large tracts at auctions still were interested in the dollar, of course, but their methods of acquiring it proved more reputable, more generous, more cognizant of the buyer.

In the upcoming crush, now seen as still another "boom" in St. Petersburg, land developers not only cleared their acreage and built roads before making their sales pitch, they also put up homes — model homes, sometimes even recreation centers, at times a series of small commercial buildings labeled on the plat as a "shopping center."

Houses changed shape, too. The two and three-story homes of years ago, with their narrow lots that ran deep to accommodate a cow, garden, cistern and barn, now gave way to wider but shallower lots. Houses were one story, built of concrete block with terrazzo floors, and made air tight for automatic cooling machines. A patch of grass outdoors was sufficient yard. Sometimes even that green swatch proved too much for folks so they became dwellers in still another creation — the "high rise."

Out of this new life-style came St. Petersburg's first shopping centers. Unlike the already burgeoning Webb's City, a sprawling complex of stores owned by an individual, the new centers contained scores of separately owned shops. Among them were Central Plaza on the south side (and later also the north side) of Central Avenue at 34th Street, and Tyrone Shopping Center at Ninth Avenue and 58th Street North.

They were mini-downtowns often built adjacent to another innovation, the housing subdivisions such as Eagle Crest, Leslee Heights, Sheryl Manor, South Causeway Isles, Disston Manor, Seminole Gardens, Ridgewood Grove, Allendale, Meadowlawn, Bahama Shores, Broadwaters, and Maximo Moorings, to name a few.

As its population hit 96,738 in 1950, St. Petersburg was spread out all over the southern end of the peninsula. And before the 1950s ended, the city would have 30 shopping centers, and 10 new banks, not to mention its third new jail, a concrete monolith at First Avenue North and 13th Street.

Academia found the city's new stability and metropolitan size ideal to its goals with the result Stetson College of Law in 1954 took over the boomday Rolyat Hotel, and Florida Presbyterian College announced it would open a four-year institution at the Maritime Base. (In 1963 it built a campus off 34th Street South and changed its name to Eckerd College.)

Notable as these improvements were, none compared to the herculean project of the Sunshine Skyway.

Point Pinellas, forever landlocked at its southern end, was a frustration to the Indians, the Spaniards, the early settlers, the town's founders, in fact, to every inhabitant who at one time or another for whatever reason wanted to go south. In 1954 the long-envisioned link was in place.

The Skyway soared gracefully over Tampa Bay from Pinellas County, across the Hillsborough

Sunshine Skyway under construction.

County portion of the bay, and touched down 15 miles later on the shores of Manatee County.

In all, it took 15 years to build, counting the establishment of a Port Authority in 1939 to plan the span. Construction didn't begin until 1949. The cost was $21 million to complete the miles of causeway, the five bridges and the 150-foot high main span.

To maintain it, a toll of $1.75 was collected from each passenger car. Four years later, after the traffic proved so voluminous, the toll was dropped to $1. In 1966, it was lowered again, to 50 cents.

When the 1950s were reviewed, chroniclers of the city's history were surprised by the what the decade had reaped. For one, St. Petersburg had begun the 10-year run overbuilt, that is, it had more houses than buyers. The 1950s ended the same way because land developers had continued subdividing and building. Yet the city's population had doubled, from 96,738 to 181,298. In 1959, for example, builders raced ahead with 3,539 new single-family dwellings in a year when 3,500 such houses already remained unsold. One result was St. Petersburg stood out among most American cities in home ownership with more than 72 percent of its citizens owning a homestead.

Also of note was the type of newcomer and home buyer in the decade. For the first time younger families dominated the influx of residents. They had come to build a life, not to retire one. With them, and following them, came new light industries, new shops, new businesses, new ideas, and above all, more children, leading to the construction of new schools and hiring of more teachers.

In retrospect, the decade of the 1950s was one of the city's best. It recorded not only an overall steadfast economy but it put down a younger population base on which the 1960s could build. Planners wasted no time. With uncommon gusto, they rushed into the next decade with a truckload of cornerstones.

Putting together a Capital Improvement Program and an Area Improvement Program, one for long-range, one for projects needing immediate attention, the city took its tools first to the downtown marina. With $800,000, it revamped and expanded the facilities, providing berths for 389 boats. A half block away, a classical $1-million Museum of Fine Arts primped for its Grand Opening in 1965.

Long outgrown was the small Mirror Lake public library. So another million-dollar check was written for a spacious, modernistic archive of books next to a small lake three miles west of downtown. It seemed distant at the time, but geographically the site today is at the approximate center of St. Petersburg.

Heavy construction equipment criss-crossed town in a dizzying pace, most of it eventually congregating at the biggest civic project undertaken in the 1960s, the Bayfront Center. Drawing against a budgeted $4.5 million, workmen erected an 8,000-seat arena and a 2,200-seat theater, all under one roof.

Inside, the versatile floor plan accommodated basketball games, ice skating, political rallies, stage spectaculars, opera, motion pictures, religious revivals, hot-mealed banquets, exhibitions and fairs, even the "Greatest Show on Earth."

As the pace quickened still more, things got a bit heady. Some say too heady. Architects, city planners, and civic leaders, smitten with the new edifices, decided some of the old landmarks no longer fit St. Petersburg's changing image. The Million Dollar Pier, for example, was now being described as unattractive and structurally unsound. So was the historic and ornate Florida Theater.

Even the city's famous green benches were denigrated — their rows and rows of ruminating elderly now were viewed as a downtown blight. Since World War II St. Petersburg had been having second thoughts about encouraging more retirees into the downtown. Their overwhelming presence on Central Avenue became the butt of jokes. Formation of another state social club for transplanted Ohioans or Michiganders was usually worthy of representation in the Festival of States parade. But by the 1960s many image-conscious leaders wished the bench-sitting newcomers would build a country club instead of a parade float. That mindset brought charges that St. Petersburg was getting too uppity.

As for the railroad tracks along First Avenue South, they now became an unsightly obstruction. For years the city had been pressuring the railroad to remove not only the tracks but to relocate its depot. It was an ironic dilemma considering that 70 years earlier the town had begged the railroads to bring their trains into the downtown.

In 1963, however, the railroad gave in. The last passenger train ceremoniously crept out of the city's innards to its "more suitable location," a track-ending depot hastily put up at 31st Street North and 36th Avenue.

If any remorse surfaced the day the final locomotive left downtown, it was strictly nostalgic. Not so when, in 1967, the Million Dollar Pier was razed.

One of the city's most famous landmarks, the Million Dollar Pier brought personal memories to thousands of citizens. Many couples met each other for the first time at the pier dances. In Spring each year high school students decorated the ballroom for their senior class proms. Its first-floor shops, its cards parties, its sing-alongs, its live shows from the WSUN studios, attracted not only tourists but residents.

So razing a "signature" structure that for 40 years had been everybody's most endearing recreation spot did not draw thundering applause. But city officials stuck to their decision, contending the landmark was in too much disrepair to keep. They promised a better-looking more functional building on the pier's end.

After the historic pier building was reduced to rubble, the wrecker's ball moved down to Fifth Street South and First Avenue and pummeled the Florida Theater, last of the baroque opera houses of the 1920s and 1930s. The First National Bank had its eye on the site for a parking garage.

While in the neighborhood, the wrecking ball also whacked down the Royal Palm and Tropic hotels on Fifth Street South near the First Avenue corner to make room for expansion of the *St. Petersburg Times.* Buoyed by a Pulitzer Prize in 1964 and removal of the railroad tracks in front of the *Times* building, the newspaper's owner, Nelson Poynter, put $1.8 million into a new five-story structure on the southeast corner of the intersection. He paid cash for the job, completed in 1968.

With growth demanding accompanying services, in 1967 the Federal Building, a concrete fortress named to honor former Congressman Bill Cramer, was erected on First Avenue South near the waterfront. A new State Office Building and a Judicial Building, both near City Hall, also went into service in the 1960s.

As the decade neared its end, the city's building department didn't have an empty file drawer left for its construction permits, its trade licenses, its inspectors' reports. Annual statistics revealed that between 1966 and 1969 a greater dollar volume of construction had occurred than in the combined previous four decades.

Never part of the mix in St. Petersburg was industry. Quasi-official boards were formed to entice light industry into the metropolitan area, but manufacturing of any kind was approached as a diet supplement. Sunshine and service, that was St. Petersburg. Progress was counted in numbers of swimming pools and hotels, not lathes and factories.

Some industry did come to the city in the 1960s, primarily as an outgrowth of the nation's new space programs. Honeywell, ECI, and General Electric parked on the city fringes and were duly welcomed. But their economic boost did not divert attention from a burgeoning "raze and raise" rallying directed at the city's core.

Impetus to the slogan was added when the 1970 Federal census soared to 216,232, giving the city metropolitan status. A new image seemed most proper and timely. The rollercoaster years of booms and busts, of the Depression, of two World

Wars, seemed forever gone.

Data supported such a change. The 1950s and 1960s had shown the median age of residents was getting younger. Many ex-servicemen who trained in St. Petersburg were returning with families. The two decades also revealed nearly unrestricted business and building expansion. If more was to come, more was to be done.

Thinking got big. Looking forward to the 1970s, planners unveiled a potpourri of construction, spiced by a multi-million-dollar complex across from the newly opened and popular Bayfront Center. First was to be a giant convention hotel, then an impressive new headquarters for Florida Power Corp; simultaneously, a sweep of swanky stores and shops were to be built, to be followed by parking garages, architecturally attractive, underground. Primed by city talent and money-raisers, the proposal rendering awed all who viewed it.

But the package of loans and grants and philanthropy to finance the project never surfaced. The grandiose dream disintegrated.

To a resilient St. Petersburg the setback proved to be more of a detour than a deterrent. It didn't give up; it merely downsized the plans. All agreed a convention hotel was of prime importance so the city concentrated on enticing a national chain. It succeeded in 1971 when the Hilton Hotel rose at First Street South near Bayfront Center.

Florida Power Corp. sent its congratulations but not its renewed interest in the downtown project. It saw its future farther west. In 1972, the corporation moved its desks and files to a new headquarters building on 34th Street South.

Taking some of the sting out of losing a corporate giant in the downtown was a celebration in 1973 at the Million Dollar Pier. Its new recreation palace was dedicated. More fanciful than the original, the modern inverted pyramid structure did not earn unanimous applause. Oldtimers thought it too glitzy, musing that it really was not conducive to the popular sing-along nights that filled the old pier building.

Nevertheless, the upended pyramid became the St. Petersburg's top-selling scenic post card.

The National Municipal League liked it, too, for that same year it named St. Petersburg an "All-American City." Two years later, in 1975, the Christian Science Monitor honored St. Petersburg as one of the 10 "most livable cities" in the U.S.

Part of the city's national attraction always has been its long history of Spring training baseball. The sport has strong supporters in town and they saw to it that facilities for the Major League teams and fans were worthy of the game. Thus, when the tired old wooden grandstand at Al Lang Field in 1975 was going into extra innings, it was dismantled and replaced by a refreshing "every-seat-has-an-unobstructed-view" new Al Lang Stadium.

But bad news came down from Beach Drive in 1974. The venerable Vinoy Park Hotel announced it was closing. Response was mixed. A spa for the well-heeled, Vinoy's Winter clientele seldom mixed with the downtown populace and therefore had minimum impact on the year-round business. Yet, the hotel graced the waterfront like a dowager aunt. It always rated a feature photo in city brochures promoting St. Petersburg. It gave the city class.

No one called for the wrecker's ball, but the Vinoy's closing did prompt an auction of the hotel's valuables. For the hoi polloi, it was an opportunity to stroll the hotel's vast foyers, to lounge about the alcoved dining rooms, perhaps even to take home a souvenir. Nearly everything went on the block – crystal light fixtures, golden sconces, dining room silver, beds, mattresses, wicker settees, even the front desk bell that summoned bellhops. When the sale was finally gaveled closed, workmen busily taped brown wrapping paper over the windows to ward off rug-fading sunlight during the structure's uncertain future.

Replacing it in 1975 as the most prestigious address in town was a new 28-story condominium, the Bayfront Towers, at the foot of Central Avenue.

Occupants of the Towers' east and south facades that year could take their martinis out on their balconies and leisurely watch the reconstruction of South Mole into a manicured yacht basin and park. Dedicated as Demens' Landing, it honored the 19th Century Russian credited with naming St. Petersburg.

The Towers' upper floors provided a cloudless view of a host of changes to the skyline in the late 1970s. To the south, a brick monolith that generated electricity for the city, the Bayboro Power Plant, was being demolished. Near its base, the city's visionaries ceremoniously were breaking ground for a University of South Florida branch campus. Toward the west, one could watch rubble dust rise from the southeast corner of Central Avenue and Fourth Street during the scheduled toppling of the 54-year-old Hall Building.

As the decade's end neared, historic buildings tumbled on schedule almost in rhythm with foundations being driven into limerock as the city continued to morph.

Not encouraging, however, was the traffic pattern on Central Avenue. More cars were heading west rather than east. Shoppers had discovered Tyrone Square Mall, passing the ailing Central Plaza Shopping Center on their way. None, of course, stopped in the Ninth Street area for Webb's City bargains. Its 70-plus stores had closed in 1979.

Coliseum decorated for Festival of States.

Taking stock, the city wasn't sure just what it had accomplished in the 1970s. It did capture a Hilton Hotel but it lost the Vinoy. The I-275 leg of Interstate 75 funneled cars through St. Petersburg but no large numbers turned off onto the exits leading downtown. Webb's City's demise pleased some downtown merchants because they expected more trade. But most of Doc Webb's customers took their business to the convenient and free parking malls of Tyrone, Northeast, Pinellas Park, and Gateway.

Downtown movie theaters and restaurants also suffered. People ate their meals and sought their entertainment near where they now shopped. Only the venerable Coliseum kept packing them in for weekend dances.

Everyone noticed that the action no longer was downtown. When offices and banks closed at 5 p.m. it was akin to a curfew that permitted no one on the streets after working hours. Another tack was to be tried in the 1980s.

Outside experts specializing in decaying downtowns were brought in. St. Petersburg, noted the city's leaders, needed a reincarnation.

Many cities across the country, not just St. Petersburg, were seeking a cure to downtown's ennui. Places like Baltimore chose to reinvigorate by converting its waterfront into one huge outdoor stadium of shops and attractions; St. Petersburg's waterfront was too sacrosanct for that treatment, but planners were amenable to retreating a few blocks back from the waterfront and pulverizing both sides of Central Avenue.

Before buying into any prescription, the city asked professional planners to assess existing problems. Their critiques included the observations that civic leaders were too fragmented in their long-range plans, that adequate parking existed but was inefficiently distributed, that city regulations stood in the way of creating a vibrant and bustling mecca.

As an example, the national clairvoyants marveled at St. Petersburg's wide streets and year-round pleasant climate, yet found no outdoor cafe dining. They discovered city codes forbade partaking of a glass of wine or coffee and donuts along streetside.

Eventually, the city hired a Kansas City firm to perform a facelift on six downtown blocks of rundown real estate. The project was tagged Bay Plaza.

In fits and starts, the skyline exhibited modest changes. Some renovations came from the Bay Plaza drawing board while others were independent of it.

Soon, the city had a new commercial complex called Jannus Landing on Central Avenue's north side. Across the street rose an imposing office and parking plaza. Near Bayboro, the Salvador Dali Museum was built, followed by the Poynter Institute, and the Great Explorations Museum. Even the Bayfront Center, only 20 years old, underwent the scalpel in a massive renovation.

Not forthcoming, however, was Bay Plaza's *creme de la creme* — a collection of upscale shops and restaurants not unlike, on a smaller scale, southern California's Rodeo Drive.

The project slowed. And it kept changing. The initial euphoria for the costly and monumental makeover waned. The Kansas City firm wanted extensions of time. In turn, the city also asked for more time to reevaluate the entire project.

By the time 1990 arrived, money for further renovations was being sponged up by a longtime city goal, getting a Major League baseball team. To entice one, the city built the Suncoast Dome (renamed the ThunderDome in 1993) in the former "gas plant" area. Before and after its completion in 1990, city sportsmen pitched existing teams around the country to move to St. Petersburg. Success came in 1995 when a new franchise was awarded, to be known as the Tampa Bay Devil Rays.

While awaiting start of the team's inaugural season in 1998, the dome catered to a variety of professional sporting events, including play by the Florida Lightning, a new National Hockey League franchise also assigned to the Tampa Bay area. The dome had the effect on downtown that many predicted — nightlife began returning to the city's core. Sports fans often stopped over at Jannus Landing just a few blocks away for a drink and snack before motoring back to their neighborhoods.

Not so pretty a sight was the 1992 demolition, by explosion, of the once-proud Soreno Hotel on Beach Drive. Its destruction had been scheduled as part of the Bay Plaza project. A growing

SORENO HOTEL

ST. PETERSBURG, FLORIDA

ON TAMPA BAY

league of history buffs campaigned to save the Soreno, which was the city's first $1-million hotel. But the protesters' efforts were too late, and too weak, as they had been for two decades when trying to stop destruction of other landmarks.

Preservationists did get some solace, however, from new owners of the nearby Vinoy Park Hotel. It was announced the Grand Dame would soon reopen in a splendor matching its original debut of 1925.

This tit-for-tat scenario occurred again in 1995. Residents still were upset by the earlier closure of their favorite department store, Maas Brothers, when the block-long building reopened as the Florida International Museum. Its inaugural exhibit, a dazzling display of priceless jewels from the days of the last Russian Czar, reaped international publicity.

Soon, such accomplishments as securing baseball and hockey franchises, a re-generated Vinoy, and a widely acclaimed new cultural museum brought into question the continued need and expense of the Bay Plaza project. To reinforce that doubt, one had only to view the corner of Beach Drive and Second Avenue North, the site of the former Soreno Hotel; after six years it remained no more than a vacant field.

Noting the 20th Century was closing fast, some movers and shakers decided to sit down and catch their breath. Not on a green bench, perhaps; that image had been pretty well erased. Nor to dwell on misdirected enthusiasm in decades past, such as the razing of historic landmarks that today would be priceless treasures.

Rather, to put one's ear to the ground, to learn the city's history. In 100 years, St. Petersburg had traveled far. Only a few generations ago the town's pioneer women were pulling weeds from Williams Park, the little Orange Belt locomotive was strain-ing out on the wooden pier trying to reach the tourists disembarking from a steamer. Still echoing in the memories of a few oldtimers are the cheering crowd at the water-front as Tony Jannus flew to Tampa in his airboat, the hawking sounds of real estate salesmen peddling lots during the booming Twenties, the operatic voice of Gladys Cornell leading a sing-along at the Million Dollar Pier, the rhythmic beat of army boots march-ing down Central Avenue during World War II basic training.

The 20th Century, for St. Petersburg, was remarkably fruitful. From a penin-sula of palmetto scrub and deserted waterfront its people had carved out and built one of the nation's most attractive and envied cities... and as Dr. Van Bibber forecast more than a century earlier, one of the healthiest.

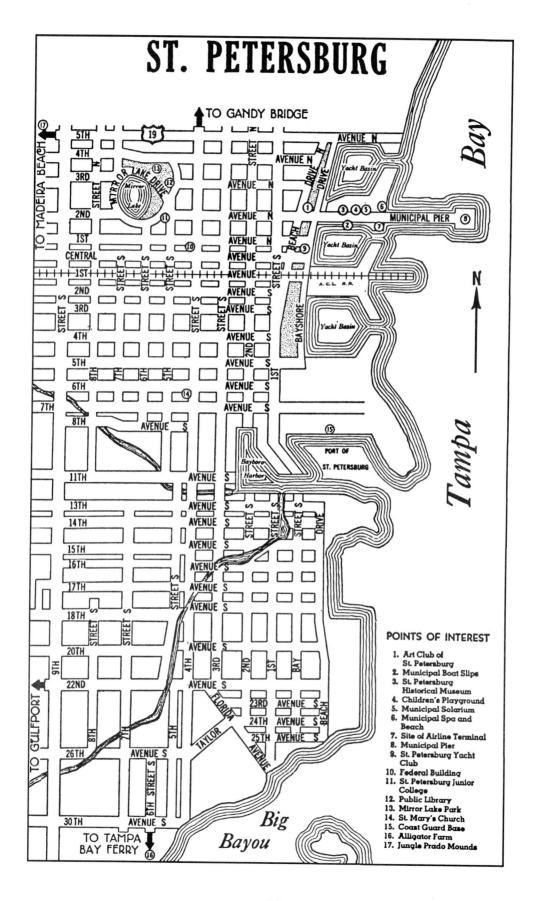

ST. PETERSBURG

TO GANDY BRIDGE

TO MADEIRA BEACH

Bay

Tampa

N

POINTS OF INTEREST

1. Art Club of
   St. Petersburg
2. Municipal Boat Slips
3. St. Petersburg
   Historical Museum
4. Children's Playground
5. Municipal Solarium
6. Municipal Spa and
   Beach
7. Site of Airline Terminal
8. Municipal Pier
9. St. Petersburg Yacht
   Club
10. Federal Building
11. St. Petersburg Junior
    College
12. Public Library
13. Mirror Lake Park
14. St. Mary's Church
15. Coast Guard Base
16. Alligator Farm
17. Jungle Prado Mounds

TO GULFPORT

TO TAMPA
BAY FERRY

Big
Bayou

AVENUE N

AVENUE N

Yacht Basin

MUNICIPAL PIER

Yacht Basin

Yacht Basin

BAYSHORE

A.C.L. R.R.

PORT OF
ST. PETERSBURG

Bayboro
Harbor

FOR ITS MORE THAN 100 YEARS St. Petersburg's main intersection has been Central Avenue and Fourth Street. In the late 1890s that intersection (*above*), with a soaring flag pole, was a sand trap in dry weather and a quagmire after a rain. The view is looking east toward the waterfront. Rutted by wagon wheels, the Central Avenue surface failed to improve with the hauling of sawdust from a lumber yard out on Ninth Street to fill the ruts. In 1897 the town turned to laying shell along the avenue. When that proved less than ideal the avenue in 1904 was bricked. Building lots in this area went for $50-to-$100, and city founder John C. Williams insisted that all new buildings be painted to dress up the town's appearance. Power lines shown are new, the first electric generating plant having just been built at the east end of Central on the waterfront.

(Facing Page) Work Progress Administration map — 1939.

THE TOWN'S FIRST SIGNIFICANT BUILDING, the Detroit Hotel (*at left*), was not the center of activity back in 1888 when the town first was platted. More development occurred on Central Avenue out at Ninth Street. One reason was "The Swale," on Central between Third and Second streets, in front of the Detroit. Described as a large depression that filled with several feet of water after a heavy rain, "The Swale" often made Central impassable. The town council, without funds, eventually took out a loan to haul dirt to the site. Once "The Swale" was filled in, the area became more attractive to Ninth Street shopkeepers. They also noticed that the new railroad terminal on the waterfront and the steamer lines were bringing people into lower Central Avenue, boosting business there. So Ninth Street folks slowly moved eastward. Among them were the Harrison brothers, who established the St. Petersburg Cash Store (*foreground at right*) on the southeast corner of Third Street and Central. The lone figure shown above emphasizes the width of the town's streets. The story handed down is that founder Williams insisted on wide streets for St. Petersburg after seeing developer Hamilton Disston carving out wide streets at his Disston City (later to become Gulfport).

PRIOR TO 1900 THE TOWN'S WATERFRONT was an unsightly and smelly disaster. The odor of rotting fish and plants along the waterfront wafted up Central Avenue. When the town was platted, 12 waterfront lots 400 feet wide and 1,000 feet deep were included, but their owners did little to dress up their property to "comport with a live, progressive city," as one historian put it. Instead, the waterfront became a collection of rickety shacks and lean-tos. Acquiring the waterfront was a goal of the town council as far back as 1888 but it had no funds to buy the land. Stepping in was the Board of Trade, a predecessor to the Chamber of Commerce. Organized in 1905, it began purchasing waterfront property to hold in trust for the time when the town could afford to buy it. It was a foresighted, magnanimous venture that led to St. Petersburg 100 years later owning the entire downtown waterfront for public use.

A TOURIST TOWN SINCE ITS BEGINNING, St. Petersburg never has been short of hotels. Its first, the Detroit Hotel (*above*) on Central Avenue between Second and Third streets, is still taking in guests at its original site a century later. It was built with 100 rooms in 1888; an expansion in 1914 added another 60 rooms. In the 1890s Central and First Street was a prime location. The Paxton (*facing page, top*) was built in 1890 at the intersection's northwest corner. Across the street, on the southwest corner, was the Claraden (*facing page, below*), built in 1894. It was owned by Dr. W. C. Van Bibber, who headed the American Medical Society study that concluded Point Pinellas was the nation's healthiest location. He lost the Claraden in 1899 when it was destroyed by fire. In fewer than 20 years after St. Petersburg's two-square-mile town was platted, more than eight hotels, offering nearly 700 rooms, had been built.

OF THE MANY DEPOTS that served the city's various railroads, none was designed with such appealing detail as its first, the Orange Belt Depot *(above)*. This charming structure, along with the Detroit Hotel, were the only major buildings near the waterfront in 1888. The depot was a half block south of Central between Second and Third streets. The Orange Belt tracks continued past its depot out onto a 3,000-foot-long railroad pier extending into Tampa Bay to serve steamer traffic. With its narrow gauge tracks, the Orange Belt was a rough ride and lasted seven years before it was leased to Henry Plant in Tampa and renamed. In 1902 the Plant system merged with the Atlantic Coast Line. One of the ACL's first locomotives *(right)* is shown arriving in St. Petersburg.

BRANTLEY'S PIER OFF SECOND AVENUE NORTH was the town's first recreation pier. A contractor with waterfront property, D. S. Brantley built the above pier in 1896 and equipped it with a bath pavilion and later a toboggan slide. It also was a commercial venture for Brantley. Besides the fun features, the pier included tracks down its center used by horse-drawn wagons that hauled freight from ships docked at the pier's end. The pier later was purchased by F. A. Davis and lengthened to accommodate large ships wishing to tie up offshore of the young town.

FAR CRY FROM A TOURIST TOWN is St. Petersburg in the late 19th Century. The view is from the crude railroad pier running out to Tampa Bay and looking west down First Avenue South. Billowing smoke is from the ice plant at the corner of First Avenue South and Second Street. The waterfront was such a disgrace at this time that town leaders began advocating public ownership. The idea was not unanimous, however, some residents advocating that it be developed into a commercial port.

THE CONSTRUCTION SUPPLY COMPANY of its day was on First Avenue South between Seventh and Eighth streets. Called the St. Petersburg Novelty Works, its owner was A. C. Pheil who went on to build the Pheil hotel and theater about 20 years after the above photo was taken around 1900. The novelty works, one of the town's largest employers, advertised brick, clay, roofing, doors, sash, screening, lath, and shingles. The building gave way in 1905 to a remodeled passenger depot for the Atlantic Coast Line railroad.

STREETCARS SERVED THE CITY'S TRANSPORTATION needs for nearly 50 years.
The first trolley cars *(above)* in 1905 cruised up and down Central Avenue to Ninth
Street, just seven years after the city acquired its initial electric generation plant.
Automobiles were coming into vogue but many folks not using the trolley still came to
town by horse and buggy. The trolley is shown in front of the Wood building on the
northwest corner of Central Avenue and Third Street. Built in 1901, the building was
only the second in the city to be made of brick. Occupying the ground floor in the early
1900s was a remnant store run by sisters Beulah and Lena Chase. Regularly expanding
the store, the sisters later joined with E. B. Willson and created Willson-Chase, for half
a century a major downtown department store.

BOARDING HOUSES WERE AS POPULAR as hotels in early St. Petersburg. This one, an ornate structure at 127 First Avenue North, began as the private residence of Col. C. F. Livingston, a town councilman in 1893. Many of the fine homes built in St. Petersburg during the period were large frame houses rising two-to-three stories, sporting gables and gingerbread. A striking feature often included a steepled roof that might provide shelter for a widow's walk. Few remain. One that does is the home built in 1890 by town founder J. C. Williams. Still on its original site on Fourth Street and Fifth Avenue South, it now operates as the Manhattan Hotel.

EARLY TROLLEYS WERE NOT SPACIOUS *(above)* but offered plenty of fresh air. They seated fewer than 20 riders. From the first day's trolley in 1905 to 1909, the line lost money. Yet investors in Disston City, Bayboro, and the North Shore pleaded for trolley service and willingly bore the expense of additional lines. More distant lines such as those heading west on Central *(below)* passed through little more than orange groves. In later years a trolley transfer station was built in the middle of Sixth Street North between Central and First Avenue. A pair of hooked-together wheelless trolleys permanently anchored in the roadbed, the station was finally removed in 1944.

THE MOST EAGERLY ANTICIPATED EVENT of the school year for children a century ago was the observance of George Washington's birthday. The above parade took place in 1910. Begun in 1896, the celebration called for area school children to plan their parts in the annual parade and create skits to be performed in the Opera House on Central Avenue. Unfortunately, rehearsing took too much of the children's time, said school officials, and in 1913 they forbade further participation by school children. The parade's continued success also was marred by Union and Confederate veterans refusing to march together. But the annual celebration survived, and in 1917 it was reincarnated as the Festival of States.

BEING A TOURIST MECCA, St. Petersburg photographers converted thousands of images of the city to post cards. A card cost a penny and so did the stamp to mail it. This photograph taken shortly before World War I was of the crowd gathering for an annual parade along Central Avenue, and became a popular post card, perhaps because it promoted the city's wide streets and its summer-like appearance. During this period, St. Petersburg had become a Spring training site for Major League baseball teams and the Open-air Post Office had just been dedicated.

BANKS WERE LITTLE NEEDED in the town during the late 1800s. The first one that did organize, the St. Petersburg State Bank, collapsed nine years later. A second, the West Coast Bank, started up in 1902 on the southeast corner of Central and Second Street. Neither looked as much like a bank, however, as the town's third bank, Central National Bank *(above)*. It occupied the southwest corner of Central and Fourth Street, a lot purchased for $5,000. Ten years later, bank deposits totaled $5 million. A review of the city's history reveals a bank has occupied this site ever since.

THE CITY WAS ABOUT TO EXPERIENCE a small boom when the Poinsettia Hotel opened at the end of 1911. Promoted as a modern hostelry, the Poinsettia was on the south side of Central Avenue just west of Fourth Street. It opened only a month after Point Pinellas was divided from Hillsborough County. Ratified by the state legislature, the division created Pinellas County, the state's 48th. In celebration, developer Walter Fuller platted new subdivisions farther west on Central, certain that the changed political status would result in added growth. C. Perry Snell and J. C. Hamlett also decided it was time to launch their North Shore development. St. Petersburg, nicknamed the "Sunshine City" just the year before by *Independent* newspaper publisher Lew Brown, was populated at the time by fewer than 4,000. That was about to nearly quadruple, to more than 14,000 before the 1920 census.

A ONE ROOM wooden schoolhouse in 1888 for 29 pupils quickly proved inadequate for the new town what with "the continual dropping in of new pupils," complained the teacher. Then as now, bond issues were the solution for new schools. One of the most attractive ever built in the city was the 1911 St. Petersburg High School *(above)*, costing $28,000, at Second Avenue North and Fifth Street. Known variously as the Grammar School and the Junior College, it was razed in 1948 for a new County Building. A temporary stage at the entrance was used for performances *(below)* during the 1912 Washington Birthday celebration.

TO ALL WHO SAW IT, St. Petersburg's waterfront was considered a natural port. The town tried for years to capitalize on that fact, dredging deepwater channels and building piers into Tampa Bay for docking ships. Of course, before the railroad arrived in 1888, the town was dependent on shipping for its supplies. Even with the arrival of the Orange Belt railroad, commercial shipping of freight and passengers continued. Perhaps the largest vessel on the run between Tampa and St. Petersburg was the *Favorite*, brought into the area from New York. It could carry 500 passengers. To accommodate the *Favorite*, F. A. Davis, who built the waterfront electric generating plant, replaced Brantley's recreation pier with a 3,000-foot long structure called the "Electric Pier" (it was lighted and electric trolley tracks extended to the pier's terminus). But already established Hillsborough County shipping interests, and Tampa's political clout, thwarted St. Petersburg's efforts to become a major harbor. Slowly, commercial shipping to St. Petersburg decreased, partly because of increased railroad traffic and partly because Gandy Bridge provided easy access to the peninsula. By 1924, St. Petersburg's watercraft traffic had switched from freight and passenger ships to pleasure crafts.

THE CITY'S PERPETUAL SUNSHINE was good for tourism but it also heated up shops and faded windowed merchandise to the extent that most downtown businesses extended awnings out over the sidewalk. In later years and during the off-season, merchants and hoteliers turned to brown paper wrapping. When hotels and shops closed in summer, for example, owners taped brown paper over all their windows, to be removed when the tourist season picked up again in Winter. The above photo was taken in 1910 looking east on Central Avenue from between Fifth and Fourth Streets. Sign at street level on building with flag is the Winston S. Branning Shoe and Clothing Store. To its right is J. G. McCrory advertising, "Nothing over 10 cents in this store."

FRESH FLOWERS AND AMERICAN FLAGS graced nearly every float or vehicle in the city's annual celebration, usually held in February at the height of the tourist season. This entry prior to World War I drew special attention by using an ostrich for power. Many parade entries were from popular tourist societies that began in 1902 with the forming of the Illinois Society. Soon tourists and residents formed societies from, in order, Michigan, Wisconsin, New York, New Jersey, Pennsylvania, Canada, Ohio, Indiana, and Iowa. Each society held regular socials or excursions, and when their members returned North, they proved to be excellent promoters of the Sunshine City. Membership of the societies totaled 12,000 at their peak in 1924.

SUPPORTING THE VIEW OF MANY TODAY that city pioneers and early residents were a hardy lot, as well as sartorially conscious, are photos such as this one, taken in 1911. Wandering Central Avenue at Fourth Street in a beating sun, women wore full-length layered dresses and plumed chapeaus while the men outfitted themselves in suits, vests, and ties. In many cases, the clothing also was of the hottest color, black. During the early decades, the women found time outside the kitchen to improve the appearance and comfort of the growing city. Their organized complaints about sand and muddy walkways that soiled their hems prompted installation of wooden sidewalks. They also landscaped Williams Park. By 1901, the women had become so enthused, and effective, that they formed the influential Woman's Town Improvement Association.

THE SOUTH SIDE OF ST. PETERSBURG developed more slowly than did the north and west sides. As this photo taken in 1913 reveals, houses and commercial buildings were widely scattered in the southeast section of town. The scene is from the First Avenue South rooftop of the just completed La Plaza Theater that fronted on Central Avenue at Fifth Street. Near the center of the photo is a 137-foot tower sometimes called the Marconi tower. It was built by E. H. Tomlinson at his home on Fourth Street South and Second Avenue. A friend of inventor Marconi, Tomlinson participated with the Italian in wireless telegraph experiments. The two-story building at center left is the St. Petersburg *Independent* newspaper. The tall, dark, four-story structure on waterfront just to right of pier is the West Coast Inn, which became a popular hotel for baseball players when Al Lang Field was later built across the street. Explaining the slow development to the south of Central Avenue, builder Walter Fuller cited three major reasons: the area had the social stigma of being "across the tracks" (the railroad tracks ran along First Avenue South), vast Lake Maggiore prevented building of through streets to the south, and the south peninsula effectively dead ended at Tampa and Boca Ciega Bays.

THE TROLLEY SYSTEM aggressively expanded to meet demands from developers on the peninsula. Started in 1905, the streetcars' initial runs were along Central from the waterfront to Ninth Street, then south on Ninth to Booker Creek. The next year the line was extended to Disston City. In 1911, a line was run to the Bayboro area, a year later to Coffee Pot Bayou to accommodate North Shore development, and in the next two years as far west as the Jungle area and south to Big Bayou. Never a money-maker for F. A. Davis, the Philadelphian who started the trolley system, it eventually was purchased by the city. In 1936 the streetcars were being retired in favor of buses, and the last trolley run was in 1949. The 1913 photo above is looking west along Central Avenue from Fifth Street.

SCHEDULE:

Lv. St. Petersburg   10:00 A. M.
Arrive Tampa   .   10:30 A. M.

Leave Tampa .   .   11:00 A. M.
Ar. St. Petersburg   11:30 A. M.

Lv. St. Petersburg   2:00 P. M.
Arrive Tampa   .   2:30 P. M.

Leave Tampa .   .   3:00 P. M.
Ar. St. Petersburg   3:30 P. M.

Special Flight Trips

Can be arranged through any of
our agents or by communicating
directly with the St. Petersburg
Hangar. Trips covering any
distance over all-water routes
and from the waters' surface to
several thousand feet high AT
PASSENGERS' REQUEST.

A minimum charge of $15.00
per Special Flight.

Rates: $5.00 Per Trip.   Round Trip $10.   Booking for Passage in Advance.

NOTE—Passengers are allowed a weight of 200 pounds GROSS including hand baggage, excess
charged at $5.00 per 100 pounds, minimum charge 25 cents. EXPRESS RATES, for packages, suit
cases, mail matter, etc., $5.00 per hundred pounds, minimum charge 25 cents. Express carried from
hanger to hanger only, delivery and receipt by shipper.

TIMETABLE *(above)* for the St. Petersburg-Tampa Airboat Line. The brochure refers to the "First regular Airboat Line in the World operating a regular schedule between two cities." Besides flights to Tampa at $5 one-way, special flights were offered travelers "covering any distance over all-water routes and from the waters' surface to several thousand feet high AT PASSENGERS' REQUEST." First scheduled flight on New Year's Day 1914 drew an anxious crowd to the St. Petersburg waterfront *(facing page, above)*. They watched the takeoff by pilot Tony Jannus from the basin near the Second Avenue North pier *(facing page, below)*. The trip to the landing site on the Hillsborough River in Tampa took 23 minutes, the return trip 18 minutes. The service was short-lived, however; after three months and a second airboat providing scheduled flights to Bradenton and Tarpon Springs, the venture collapsed.

FROM SILENTS TO SILENCE

In 1905 with the Royal Palm Theater, movie houses began a 60-year run along Central Avenue. Silent films were to continue at the Grand, the Star (later to be the Pheil), the Alcazar, and the opulent La Plaza, which dominated the corner of Central at Fifth Street.

As "talkies" and "ice-cooled air" were perfected in the 1920s, St. Petersburg built its Queen of Theaters, the Florida. Showing only top rate, first-run films, the Florida, just south of Central Avenue on Fifth Street, also staged live shows with stars such as Eddie Cantor, fan dancer Sally Rand, and Elvis Presley.

Cost to build the 2,500-seat "exotic Occidental" Florida Theater was $1 million, a tidy sum in 1926. But cinema fans got every dollar's worth. Oh, some patrons sniffed that the Florida was too gaudy, too overdressed, with its tufted velvet, candleflame lights and gilt mirrors. But to impressionable movie fans, already enchanted by the fantasy world of screen star sheiks and exotic locations, the Florida Theater was a magic carpet. A hint of Tara swept up the red-carpeted staircase; a glint of golden Camelot reflected off tapestries and crested shields.

It is possible that every young girl in St. Petersburg wondered at some time just how royal she might feel to sit, even for a moment, in one of those stage-side box seats framed by columns and carved, winged lions. In reality, those enviable box seats were not seats at all, but lofts of pipes for the mighty Giant Concert Wurlitzer organ, a music machine capable of blowing fans back into the lobby.

The Florida Theater's reign extended from 1926 until the early 1960s, when suburban shopping centers began opening their unadorned viewing caves — little more than candy shops that incidentally screened films, predecessors of today's "multi-plexes." This change adversely affected all of St. Petersburg's downtown theaters.

In 1962, however, on Central Avenue a block from the Florida, the Center Theater (formerly the Roxy) bought some time by installing the city's first wide, wide movie screen and ear-splitting sound system. There, stretching across the theater's full width, Lawrence of Arabia aimed his camel across palpably hot sands as the film's haunting theme swelled to full crescendo. Three years later, balilaika music swept Lara into the icy arms of Doctor Zhivago.

The Center's technology proved to be only a temporary stay attraction. If beautiful films were back, beautiful movie houses were not. By then, the Florida Theater's gilt was fading and carpets were threadbare. The magnificent velvet curtains had not parted for a live, onstage performance since the 1965 Bayfront Center construction. Now treated more like a harlot than a belle, the Florida was proving an unprofitable palace.

Many citizens were horrified at the first whispers of the Florida's demise. Surely, there was no plan to demolish the once-glorious, historical structure.

But she was doomed. Saddened fans quietly assembled in 1967 to watch the wrecking ball career into the Florida's ribcage. Spunky to the end, it took days to bring her crashing down.

The grand theater's site became...what else...a parking lot.

BEFORE WORLD WAR I slowed down the growth of St. Petersburg, the city sometimes became one traffic jam with nearly every type of conveyance in use. Shown is the intersection of Central Avenue and Fifth Street in 1915. Motor cars were gaining in popularity, the trolley line was busy enough to require tandem streetcars, and some folks still came into the downtown in horse and buggy. The view is looking southeast with the La Plaza Theater on the right, a four-story bank building to its left, and next to the bank the Hotel Poinsettia.

SHELL MOUND PARK was one of the last surviving of some seven Indian mounds discovered on Point Pinellas when the white settlers moved in. Indians built several types of mounds, including temple mounds often for the chief's house, burial mounds, and midden mounds that were comprised of mainly shells and garbage. Shell Mound was at Seventh Street South and Sixth Avenue, where St. Petersburg's first full-fledged hospital, Augusta Memorial, was built *(above)*. The mound was eventually leveled for hospital expansion. Augusta Memorial became City Hospital and in 1923 Mound Park Hospital.

ONCE CONSIDERED A SHOWPLACE MANSION was the home of C. W. Springstead at 256 Beach Drive. A Wisconsin native, Springstead came to St. Petersburg to grow citrus. When his citrus endeavors did not pay off, he turned to real estate development and created Spring Hill subdivision in the area between Fourth and Ninth streets north near Crescent Lake. His home above was built in the Queen Anne style about 1915. It was torn down in the 1960s.

FISHING IN TAMPA BAY off St. Petersburg's waterfront was a great attraction for tourists and residents, so much so that scores anchored their skiffs there and some even got permission from lot owners to nail together a shack at the shoreline. It wasn't long before the city's greatest asset looked like its biggest trash heap. This 1914 photo did not make a pretty post card promoting St. Petersburg. After the city lost its early bid to become a deepwater port, city officials for years mourned over the lack of tax money to buy up the waterfront properties and thereby save the downtown shoreline from commercialization and unmanaged use. But they persevered to the extent that by the time of its centennial year, St. Petersburg had purchased and taken control of nearly every frontage parcel from Coffee Pot Bayou on the north to Bayboro Harbor on the south.

AN OAK AND PINE WOODS, Williams Park was an early favorite picnic spot. And as improvements were made, including a fence in 1902 to keep out the cows, the park became the social core of the city. Six-foot walks criss-crossed the park, shown here in 1915. Besides a bandshell the grounds featured a fountain at its center. Just about every kind of game has been played in the park, including checkers, chess, dominoes, horseshoes, even roque. Several organizations tried getting permission at times to build a small clubhouse in the park but the idea was always vetoed by the city, its officials explaining that no one group should have special privileges in the park. The park's environs have been the scene of events ranging from political rallies to Easter parades but its most popular use for decades has been band concerts. Hundreds of out-of-state bands have performed from the park's bandshell, particularly during the Festival of States celebrations.

More automobiles in pre-World War I days warranted a policeman to direct traffic.

After a 1914 parade, the crowd breaks up along Central Avenue east of Third Street.

ONE OF THE MORE attractive hotels just north of Central Avenue before the 1920s boom was the 74-room Floronton Hotel on the southeast corner of First Avenue North and Second Street. After World II, the Floronton became the Toffenetti Hotel and its dining room was popular with downtown workers for breakfast and lunch.

UNDULATING ROSER PARK was the dream development in 1911 of C. M. Roser who began purchasing the acreage east of Ninth Street South near Ninth Avenue. At the time, Roser Park area with its creek and its hillsides was not in the city limits. By 1921 nearly 100 homes had been built in the area. It was and remains a semi-tropical beauty spot in the city, but its address never became as prestigious as the waterfront residences of Snell Isle on Coffee Pot Bayou or of Park Street along Boca Ciega Bay.

FEWER THAN 10 Carnegie-funded public libraries remain in Florida. One is the
Mirror Lake Branch Library (*above*) at Fifth Street North between Second and Third
avenues. The Neo-classic structure was built in 1915 for $17,500 and has been in
continuous use, abetted by additions. When city population growth demanded much
larger facilities, a new main library was built west of downtown on Ninth Avenue North.

SQUANDERING MONEY, that is what many investors and developers thought of building on the beaches. Natives particularly found the islands unappealing — plagued by mosquitoes and sand fleas, cubic yards of sand that made walking impossible, and gardens of sandspurs. Even newcomers to St. Petersburg were not attracted to the salty shore, in part because prior to World War I the only way to reach the beaches to the city's west was via trolley to Gulfport and then by boat to the islands. That changed when a colorful out-of-town huckster, W. D. McAdoo, built a wooden toll bridge from near Fifth Avenue South to the St. Petersburg Beach area in 1919. At Pass-a-Grille (*above*), a Casino was erected and several boardwalks were built to facilitate walking over the hot sand. Soon the cars showed up. Interestingly, the patrons were a new type of tourist, a younger, more energetic crowd. A few years later Welch Causeway was built, connecting the mainland around Seminole to the northern beaches.

THE PARTY DID NOT CEASE after the boom collapsed in the mid-1920s and a favorite nightspot was Spanish Bob's atop the Snell Arcade at Central Avenue and Fourth Street *(above)*. Most developers went bust around 1925 but C. Perry Snell started his towering Snell Building with its arcade of statuary in 1926. This photo was taken shortly after completion in 1929. During the 1920s, clubs and dance halls were popular in St. Petersburg. Besides Spanish Bob's were the Coliseum, the Gold Dragon at the northwest corner of Central and Fifth Street, the Green Lantern on the North Mole, and the Gangplank at Jungle Prado.

FREE CONCERTS ALL WINTER at Williams Park were a tradition that brought tourists to St. Petersburg every year. Of all the different band shells in the park, the half-moon stage in the 1920s (*above*) was its most attractive. The park has always served as the city's core, it being an oasis among surrounding hotels, restaurants, and department stores, and the destination and transfer site for people using the city bus system.

POPULAR TO THIS DAY is the shuffleboard club at Mirror Lake. The first courts were built in 1923 and membership in the club grew to more than 12,000. Its officers described the club as the largest in the world. The clubhouse and surrounding grounds have always been a meeting place for tourists. Seven years earlier a lawn bowling club was established in the area. And, as this 1920s photo shows, tourists also took their card play out into the sunshine.

AUTOMOBILES, HORSE DRAWN CARTS, AND PEDESTRIANS bustled along Central Avenue in the 1920s. Shown is a busy week day along the avenue looking east toward the waterfront from between Fifth and Fourth streets. At right is the Hotel Poinsettia. Many of the small signs along the avenue designated real estate offices. In these bygone days, a trip into town meant wearing a white shirt, tie, and even a coat.

SAND CASTLES

In the late 1920s, Cincinnati insurance magnate William J. Williams was smitten, as had been so many before him, by the beauty of St. Petersburg. Already situated in a comfortable home site overlooking Boca Ciega Bay at the corner of Park Street and Fifth Avenue North, Williams reveled in the spectacular St. Petersburg sunsets. And he wanted more.

In a bold move, Williams acquired the adjoining land owned by his neighbor Al Lang and launched the construction a two-acre dream castle to be called Casa Coe Da Sol, Home of the Setting Sun. A man of consummate taste and wealth, Williams hired architect Addison Mizner, king of Palm Beach castles, to draw up the blueprints.

Mizner had become famous during the Roaring Twenties boom. Backed by the monied "Golden Horde," from the Churchills to the Vanderbilts to Irving Berlin, Mizner fashioned romantic Spanish villas in stunning pastels and earth tones that captured, shaded, and cooled the Florida sun while providing glimpses of such foreign playgrounds as Venice, Florence, and the French Riviera.

But by the time Williams signed up Mizner, the architect's health was failing. Worse, Mizner's reputation had suffered a serious blow when advertising of Mizner's $100 million planned development of Boca Raton was labeled false and misleading — the claim being that far more was being promised than was being delivered. Financial backers fled and the Boca Raton venture halted.

Some historians point out that Florida's real estate boom had run its course and was prime for a bust, in any event. Other chroniclers, however, assert that Mizner was an adventurer and that criticism of him among the North's wealthy clientele actually killed the state's boom.

So it was under that cloud, with builder Oscar Steinert on board, that construction of the 11,000-square-foot Mizner-designed Williams residence was completed in 1931.

True to form, the home is embellished with trademark Mizner touches, including cast quarry columns, gargoyles, handmade clay tiles in "Mizner blue" turquoise, wrought iron balconies, clay tile flower pots and urns, and the signature Mizner irregular roof tiles — termed "knee" tiles because they were literally molded across a laborer's foreleg.

The interior of Casa Coe Da Sol likewise was stocked with Mizner Industry furnishings such as artificially distressed tables made to resemble "Old World" imports. Other interior detailing included a central, two-story rotunda floored in tile and topped with a blue glass ceiling. A double "flying" staircase swept to the five second floor bedrooms, one of which was Art Deco black glass trimmed in silver leaf. A powder room sported a solid goldleafed ceiling and the library's ceiling was decorated with a handpainted mural.

Sadly, Williams did not long enjoy his Mizner palace. He died in 1933. In a strange coincidence, Addison Mizner also died in 1933, leaving Casa Coe Da Sol as the last of his designs ever constructed and the only Mizner castle ever built on Florida's west coast.

A SUNNY AFTERNOON in the 1920s along Central Avenue could be a pleasant and convenient outing. Benches lined the wide sidewalk, the city's busiest drug store was nearby as was the Palmetto Cafeteria. Parking, without meters or time limits, was plentiful. Pearce's Drug even provided a free weight machine (*far right*) near its entrance. And in the evenings, the avenue was aglow from decorative street lamps.

GREYHOUND RACING came to the St. Petersburg area in 1925 with the building of the St. Petersburg Kennel Club, better known as Derby Lane. Opened on Gandy Boulevard a year after the completion of Gandy Bridge, the race track offered a clubhouse, a grandstand, and both day and night racing. Still operating, it is one of the state's oldest dog racing tracks.

"TO PROMOTE, ENCOURAGE AND PROTECT interests of boating and boatsmen in and about the City of St. Petersburg," the St. Petersburg Yacht Club was formed in 1909. Eight years later it built its clubhouse on the waterfront at Central Avenue at a cost of $15,000. (Built was the structure on the right; the wing on the left was added in 1922.) Building funds were borrowed from local banks on personal notes from members. Membership fee was $25 a year. The clubhouse survived the 1921 hurricane, which severely damaged downtown waterfront property, and the club continues to function on the site.

MAJOR LEAGUE BASEBALL Spring training has taken place in St. Petersburg since 1914, when the St. Louis Browns came to town. Since then, teams choosing the city for their training sites have included the Boston Braves, Philadelphia Phillies, New York Yankees, New York Giants, New York Mets, St. Louis Cardinals, and briefly, the Baltimore Orioles. The Spring training park on the waterfront was not built until 1922, the year of this photo showing the Boston Braves at play. Earlier, the Braves trained at a diamond built along Coffee Pot Bayou. A diamond built at Crescent Lake also was used by teams. In the above photo, at the right top, are the Spa pool and the Solarium on the approach to the still unbuilt Million Dollar Pier building, and behind the grandstand is seen the St. Petersburg Yacht Club. In 1947 the above ball park was renovated and dedicated as Al Lang Field, in honor of the city's greatest baseball booster. Then, in 1975, that facility was razed to make way for an all-new concrete grandstand and rededication as Al Lang Stadium.

JUST TWO DECADES after becoming a city, St. Petersburg had done wonders with its waterfront. In 1910 it had chosen to make its waterfront a huge public park. By 1924 *(above)*, landscaping had begun and public facilities such as the Spa pool and the Solarium *(above along pier)* had been completed. It was also the year Gandy Bridge, the Princess Martha and Soreno hotels, and the Coliseum were built. The real estate boom, at its height, wasn't to collapse for another year. The following year the Million Dollar Pier building and Vinoy Park Hotel were to be built, and by 1929 the city boasted its public waterfront holdings encompassed 90 acres.

THE SORENO HOTEL became known as the city's first hotel to cost $1 million when it opened in 1924 on Beach Drive and First Avenue North. Within one month, every one of its 300 rooms was occupied. Its owner, Soren Lund, a native of Denmark, had come to St. Petersburg to purchase the Huntington Hotel at Second Street and Fourth Avenue North, which he did, and then decided to build the Soreno. Its grandeur was to be eclipsed the next year by the $3-million Vinoy Park Hotel, but the Soreno was a favorite until it was torn down in 1992.

CELEBRITIES ENJOYED the first-class accommodations offered by the fine hotels that St. Petersburg was building facing waterfront park. Among the scores that chose to escape northern Winters for the Soreno was tennis star Helen Wills (*left*). The shaded wicker strollers, pushed along the streets by hotel porters, were comfortable and cool transportation for trips to nearby shops and for downtown sight-seeing.

THE COLISEUM, the most popular of St. Petersburg's landmarks, remains one of the South's finest ballrooms. Built in 1924 at a cost of $250,000, it has changed little over the years, the biggest renovation being the addition of air conditioning in 1955. The Coliseum was constructed on Fourth Avenue North near Mirror Lake by a promoter named Charles Cullen, but it is most identified with Rex MacDonald, who leased it in 1929. In 1944 he and his wife, Thelma, went in partnership with Mr. and Mrs. W. C. Kaleel and purchased the Coliseum. A musician, MacDonald brought in scores of Big Bands. He also formed his own band, the Silver Kings, and his orchestra along with Bob Burklew and his Dixians provided music for generations of dancers.

DANCING WAS NOT AN EXCLUSIVE use of the Coliseum near Mirror Lake. During economic doldrums, a variety of events were booked at the 1924 ballroom to pay expenses. When Big Bands weren't available, owner Rex MacDonald scheduled banquets, wrestling and boxing matches, tennis tournaments, even appearances by the likes of evangelist Aimee Semple McPherson. For decades the Festival of States has held its annual Coronation Ball at the Coliseum. In the 1980s, devotees of the Coliseum got a scare when talk circulated about the Coliseum being torn down. The city chose not to lose the landmark so in 1989 it purchased the Coliseum... and the band played on.

LOOKING SOUTHEAST TOWARD BAYBORO Harbor in 1924. The photo was taken from atop the Pheil building on Central Avenue near Fourth Street. Street in foreground running across photo is Second Avenue South and street at right running south is Fourth Street. Acreage beyond Bayboro Harbor eventually became the Coquina Key housing development. On Fourth Street is seen the city's Roman Catholic church at the time, built in 1916 and demolished in 1925 when St. Mary's Roman Catholic Church was built at Fourth Street South and Fifth Avenue.

THE FIRST SCHOOLS IN ST. PETERSBURG clustered around the Mirror Lake area. The finest at the time was *(above)* a two-story brick schoolhouse first used as St. Petersburg Normal and Industrial school. Later it became St. Petersburg Normal and High School, and later Central Primary. In 1946 it was closed and eventually made way for the County Building at Fifth Street North and Second Avenue.

EARLY SCHOOL BUS was called a "Jitney Bus" and in 1920 was under contract to the School Board to haul students from outlying districts. The board chose not to own buses.

A FIXTURE IN DOWNTOWN has been Florida Power Corp. It built this headquarters at First Avenue South and Fifth Street in 1925. By the 1970s, the corporation needed larger quarters and planned to become part of a major downtown renovation project that would include a major hotel, swanky shops, new office buildings, and increased parking facilities. But lack of financing fragmented the massive construction project, so Florida Power officials decided to build its new headquarters building on 34th Street South. It opened in 1972.

THE CITY'S MAIN INTERSECTION was, and to many remains, Central Avenue and Fourth Street. Here it is in 1926, looking west. The trolleys remained until the late 1940s. The northwest corner, behind the trolley, is the real estate office of Noel Mitchell, a one-time mayor but more noted for putting out on the sidewalk the first green benches for which the city became famous. The corner became the site of the Snell Building. In the distance is the Kress Building, and beyond it the newly built Hotel Alexander.

BATHING IN SIGHT of the newly completed Million Dollar Pier in 1926. The pier building became the "signature" of St. Petersburg, its image appearing on post cards mailed throughout the world. Its many uses, from rooftop dancing to weekly sing-alongs to a meeting place for tourists societies, made the massive Moorish structure so popular that residents protested when the city demolished it in 1967 for a new design. The bathers are cooling off on Spa Beach, which adjoins the pier.

AN OPEN-AIR POST OFFICE befuddled Washington postal officials. When St. Petersburg built its first one (on Central Avenue and Fourth Street's northeast corner in 1907), federal officials insisted an enclosed front be added. Then-postmaster Roy Hanna argued that an open-air facility at which box holders could pick up their mail day or night fitted St. Petersburg's climate and customers. Federal officials gave in. The building soon was outgrown, however, and a new building site, on the southwest corner of First Avenue North and Fourth Street was purchased from the Congregational Church. When the cornerstone was laid in 1916, the architects said the new Open-air Post Office was large enough to serve a city of 100,000. That building (*above*) still serves patrons but now as a branch; a large main Post Office building was opened in 1957 on First Avenue North and 31st Street. The photo is looking toward the north west with the left side of the building running along an alley that was shared by the Snell Building. In the background at right is the Princess Martha Hotel. Since postmaster Hanna's time, inclement weather did affect postal workers so the alley-side of the above building was enclosed to ward off driving rains and cold spells.

EVERYTHING LOOKED BRAND NEW along the waterfront in the early 1920s, and much of it was. The city's population was only about 20,000, but tourism and the post-World War I economy were on a roll. The Ponce de Leon Hotel, front and center, was opened in 1922, the same year as the north wing on the St. Petersburg Yacht Club (*at right*). Behind the Ponce de Leon is the Soreno Hotel, opened in 1924, and out on the pier beyond the Spa Pool building at far right the Million Dollar Pier building was under construction. In the next couple years, the Vinoy Park Hotel would be finished, and developer C. Perry Snell would be dredging and filling along North Shore Park and building homes on Snell Isle *(top)*. It was in 1926 that voters approved the greatest expansion of the city limits, annexing more than 38 acres.

HANGING FROM THE ROOFTOPS to view the Festival of States parade in 1926. The view is along Central Avenue from between Third and Fourth streets looking west. The tall structure at right, on the northeast corner of Fourth Street, started out as the West Coast Title Co., then became Equitable Bank, and later Florida Federal Savings and Loan. Across the street on the southeast corner is the Hall Building, put up in 1924 (later to become Schwobilt's). The awninged building on the southwest corner is the Central National Bank, tucked next to the tall Pheil Hotel and Theater. Columns of New Hampshire-imported granite can be seen being added to the American Bank & Trust Co. at far left. The bank failed after the stock market crash of 1929 and the building later housed McKinnon Securities. For four generations, the Festival of States has paraded down Central Avenue, and is promoted as one of the South's largest civic celebrations.

ST. PETERSBURG'S MOST BEAUTIFUL BUILDING is the description often given
the Snell Building on the northwest corner of Central Avenue and Fourth Street. C.
Perry Snell, who developed the North Shore area and Snell Isle, was one of the few
developers who didn't go bankrupt when the economic boom collapsed in late 1925. He
continued to develop property and in 1926 began the Snell Building. A collector of
miniature art and a frequent traveler to Europe where he purchased statuary and
antiques, Snell used his collection of European building tile in his towering office
building, which included a ground floor arcade. The Snell Building was completed in
1929, later purchased by banker Hubert Rutland and renamed the Rutland Building.

THE SNELL ARCADE was a street-level walk-through fronting on Central Avenue beneath the Snell Building. It contained offices, a barbershop, and other service businesses, none of which had ever enjoyed such beautiful commercial space. Floors and walkways were decorated with imported tile, office fronts were carved from expensive woods, and statuary gazed down from elevated pedestals. Many people enjoyed walking through the arcade to the Open-air Post Office, which was across an alley. In photo one can see the postage window in the post office at rear of arcade. The small balcony at top led to Spanish Bob's nightclub on a roof garden of the Snell Building.

FAVORITE EN TRAYS

Decades ago, diners in St. Petersburg were of two types — those who sat down at a table to be served and those who lined up to carry a tray.

Of the two kinds of eateries, the latter, cafeterias, drew the biggest crowds. And for good reasons. Living in hotels and apartments near the city's core were thousands of elderly. Being relatively immobile, that is, lacking an automobile, they preferred taking their meals downtown. Some were on meager pensions, which dictated that they eat on the cheap, so to speak. Others, including well-heeled retirees, enjoyed the socializing that cafeteria dining provided.

Thus, cafeterias flourished in downtown St. Petersburg. Inexpensive, open at all hours, serving plain but delicious selections for all palates, the cafeterias also attracted downtown secretaries and store clerks who had only a hour or less to get their mid-day nourishment.

Everyone had his or her favorite. Among the most popular was the Orange Blossom Cafeteria on Fourth Street North near Second Avenue. Devoid of glitz and music, it drew long lines and went on to survive most of its competitors. It eventually closed to specialize in catering.

For atmosphere, if not for quality of food, the Tramor Cafeteria on Fourth Street South between First and Second avenues was unbeatable. Inside, during its heyday, up to 30 waiters would carry trays for the 2,000 daily diners. The atmosphere was always festive with live music that often prompted customers to break out in song beneath the white stucco ceiling splashed with blue to resemble a Florida sky. Said owners Enar and Lander Haige, "Some of these people, we feed them their first meal in Winter and their last one before they go back home up North in the Spring."

Tourists often nixed the Driftwood Cafeteria on the northwest corner of Fifth Street North at Second Avenue. It was too noisy, too hectic, too rushed. Responsible were the office crowds from the nearby City Hall, law offices, and shops, workers who could not afford the time to take a meal at leisure.

Lower Central Avenue diners preferred the venerable Morrison's Cafeteria on the south side of Central nearer the waterfront. A basic no frills rendition of a modern-day Morrison's, it was one of downtown's first cafeterias to open and first to go out of business.

Families often dined at Webb's Old South cafeteria. It was, by 1950s standards, downright opulent — cool, quiet, lighted with recessed pink neon, and soothed by the sweet strains of an organist. Seating 500, cafeteria diners often shopped at Webb's after dinner. Busy for breakfast, lunch, and dinner, Old South had unbeatable prices, which Doc Webb often lowered when money got tight. He also was savvy enough to know that every cafeteria diner was a potential customer at his numerous stores and departments.

The downtown cafeterias slowly disappeared when the green benches were removed and when shopping centers beckoned older folks to catch a bus and spend a day at a mall.

By the 1990s, nearly all were gone, the Driftwood being the last to be razed. Only the Tramor survived; now owned by the *St. Petersburg Times,* it serves only the newspaper's staff.

SIMULATING OUTDOOR DINING was the Tramor Cafeteria on Fourth Street South between First and Second avenues. Built in 1929 in a Spanish hacienda motif, the Tramor featured an arched sky ceiling across which passed painted clouds, a rising and setting sun, even a moon. When dark clouds hovered, musicians in the balcony struck up *Stormy Weather*. For decoration, the Tramor was lighted with stained-glass lanterns, its floors and walls made of colored tile, its recesses greened with potted plants. During World War II, it became the government's fanciest mess hall, the cafeteria being used to feed Army troops training in St. Petersburg.

NO OPENING OF A CLASS HOTEL was more ceremonious than the 1926 soiree noting the completion of the Rolyat Hotel. The Spanish-style hotel on 61st Street South near Pasadena was, newspapers reported, as handsome as its creator, Jack Taylor. Married to a monied Du Pont, Taylor arrived from New York and stayed only long enough to develop Davista (renamed Pasadena) and build the Rolyat. He conducted business out of a private railroad car, was chauffeured around town in Daimler automobiles, and brought in celebrities for the hotel's opening, including baseball's Babe Ruth and golf's Walter Hagen. The souring economy forced the hotel's closing a year after it opened. Taylor fled back to New York. Between 1932-51, the Florida Military Academy operated out of the Rolyat, and in 1954 it became home to Stetson College of Law.

AS DOWNTOWN REAL ESTATE PRICES WENT HIGHER, so did downtown buildings. Tall white structure in this 1926 photo is the Florida Theater nearing completion at Fifth Street South on the northeast corner of First Avenue. The small dark building behind power pole is the *St. Petersburg Times*. Adjoining it on its south were both the Royal Palm and the Tropic Hotels. Workers in the area took their meals at the Bombay Cafeteria shown adjacent to the *Times* building.

THE MUNICIPAL PIER'S popularity becomes clear from this photo taken in the late 1920s showing the many attractions the city placed on the extension into Tampa Bay. At top is the newly completed Million Dollar Pier building. Farther west on the left is Spa Beach, then the Spa Pool building, then the Solarium. A massive fill was added for parking and a children's playground, next to the lone white building — the St. Petersburg Historic Museum built in 1922 — at lower right. Round building in lower right corner is a restroom facility. On the pier's right or south side is the Municipal Marina with the spit of fill across from the Spa Pool first used as the terminal for airboat flights to Tampa, and later as the site of Webb's Senior Citizen Center.

A RESTFUL GETAWAY for tourists was this shaded loggia at the Million Dollar Pier building. These folks in 1928 are relaxing on the second floor's southern exposure. At left in back is stairway leading down to the main floor. The loggia encircled the entire structure, providing a panoramic elevated view across the bay, and west toward downtown.

PINELLAS POINT ADDITION, a project that never was built. In the 1920s, a residential region known as Pinellas Point, on the southern tip of the peninsula, was in the hands of Murok Realty Corp. By 1927 it had sold all but 120 residential lots in Pinellas Point and announced plans to construct "140 acres of new land, surrounded by deep canals and lagoons" and called Pinellas Point Addition. Envisioned, as shown below, was dredging and filling out beyond the existing upland (shaded area) out into Tampa and Boca Ciega bays, thereby creating residential lots fronting on canals of "from 50 feet to 250 feet wide and of sufficient depth to accommodate craft drawing four to eight feet of water, at low tide." The sales brochure spoke of "24-foot wide pavements, tinted a soft red to avoid glare and the reflection or absorption of heat." To facilitate pre-project sales, Murok had built on the Pinellas Point upland a two-story timber Administration building and a Log Cabin Tea Room in which "many lovely luncheons and dinners are served to the elite of St. Petersburg." Pinellas Point Addition never materialized, but the natural upland of Pinellas Point did become one of the city's more prominent and attractive residential areas.

PINELLAS POINT
ADDITION
ST. PETERSBURG
FLORIDA
Murok Realty Corporation
401 First Avenue, North

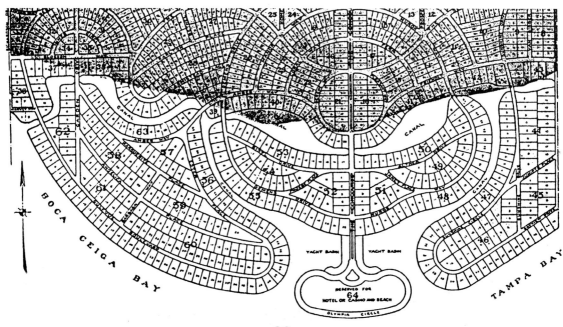

THIS PICTURE POST CARD mailed in 1927 by a tourist was found in an antique store in San Francisco. The photo shows Beach Drive near the Soreno Hotel. On the back, the sender wrote: "The white building on the corner is our resting place. It looks out on the water. We are having a wonderful winter — the mockingbirds are singing and the flowers are lovely. Wish I could send you the orange blossoms I have in the room. They scent the whole place."

STYLE OF ARCHITECTURE called Mediterranean Revival was dominant in St. Petersburg in the 1920s both in construction of homes and commercial buildings. Typical was the above southwest corner building at Second Avenue North and Second Street. It was the ticket office in 1928 for both the Atlantic Coast Line railroad and the P & O Steamship Co. Lettering on window of second floor office reads Dr. William Quicksall, Nose and Throat.

PHOTOGRAPHS WERE A PRIMARY promotional medium for developers in the 1920s and C. Perry Snell hired landbound and aerial photographers to picture his North Shore and Snell Isle projects. Purpose of the above photo is a mystery, however — a dozen black-suited men fishing from the wooden bridge across Coffee Pot Bayou. Snell's $1 million development of the Coffee Pot area began in 1911 with a trolley line, seawalls, a golf course, roads, sewers, water and gas. In the background can be seen the clubhouse of Snell's nine-hole Coffee Pot Golf Course, the city's second, which opened in January 1920. The course later was expanded to 36 holes totaling more than 12,000 yards in length and a new Sunset Golf clubhouse was built by Snell in 1928.

INFLUENCE OF THE JAPANESE style that was so popular during the 1920s is apparent in the Coffee Pot Golf Course clubhouse. Built in 1919 and later enlarged, the clubhouse provided catered meals and a Japanese garden that was considered a city showplace.

IN COST, QUALITY, AND SIZE, no development contributed more to St. Petersburg than Snell Isle, the multi-million dollar dream of C. Perry Snell. When all of Florida was reeling from the collapse of the real estate boom after 1926, Snell refused to give up on his dream of building beautiful homes and neighborhoods in the Northeast section of the city and on Snell Isle. His one-time sales manager, Walter Fuller, writes that Snell often never had more than $11 in his pocket, died a poor man on an antique buying trip to Mexico, and "deliberately impoverished himself in pursuit of beauty." Shown (*above*) is the clubhouse of the Sunset Golf Club nearing completion on Snell Isle in the late 1920s. The view is south toward the mainland. Snell Isle, after its development, encompassed some 275 acres; only 39 acres were above high tide when Snell began his project.

TWO VIEWS OF NORTHEAST St. Petersburg in late 1920s after completion of the Vinoy Park Hotel. Above, looking northeast, shows Tampa Bay fill north of the Municipal Pier. In bottom photo Vinoy is in foreground. Road through fill is North Shore Drive and thoroughfare to its west Beach Drive. The 14-acre Vinoy site sold in 1880 for $36.

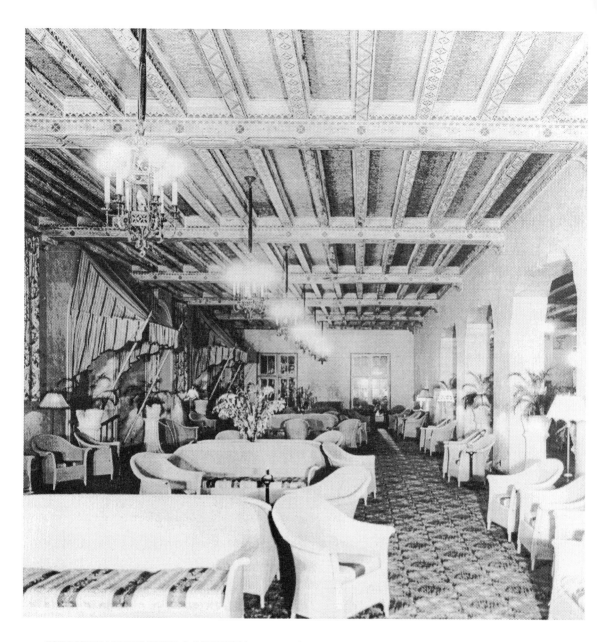

VINOY PARK HOTEL LOUNGE in 1930, five years after the hotel opening. Exquisite details in the $3-million hotel included glazed quarry tile, stenciled pecky cypress beams, and frescoed ceilings and walls. An American plan hotel, the Vinoy Park charged $20 a room the year it opened. Before it closed in disrepair in 1974, rooms were down to $7 a night. After its $93-million renovation in 1992, rates ranged between $130 and $216. The original Vinoy was open only during "the season," from December to March, and enjoyed a brisk business even during the Depression because of its elite clientele. High tea was served daily, between 4 and 6 p.m.

MAGNIFICENT LIGHT FIXTURES in the Vinoy Park Hotel lobby were suspended from the two-story vaulted ceiling by hand-tooled leather straps. Unlike conventional chandeliers, the lobby fixtures were not round nor octagonal but flat, giving the semblance of huge banners. Lighting fixtures in the loggia were designed as cages, in which were perched colorfully painted life-sized parrots. Also unique was lighting in the ballroom — the orchestra leader could change the dance floor's illumination to rose or yellow or to any color to coincide with the mood of the music. Vinoy was the middle name of its builder, Aymer Vinoy Laughner, whose Pennsylvania family became rich in the oil industry.

AMONG THE FIRST RESIDENCES built on Snell Isle was the home of developer C. Perry Snell facing south across Coffee Pot Bayou. Filled with valuable imported furnishings and building materials, it set the pace for dozens of more beautifully designed two and three-story homes along the bayou on the Isle's Brightwaters Boulevard. The Snell residence has had several owners, including cartoon-strip artist Wally Bishop, and still stands as a "signature" residence of the development.

NEVER WANTING FOR TENANTS were the Snell Isle Garden Apartments, an attractive cluster of small suites built around a courtyard. They were built in 1926, just across Coffee Pot Bayou on Snell Isle, a short 10-minute drive from downtown.

BY TROLLEY, BY CAR, BY BICYCLE, BY FOOT — thousands of residents and tourists took their recreation in the late 1920s at the Million Dollar Pier. The trolley actually went inside the pier building's first floor, where the conductor flipped the seats to face in the opposite direction, then took his portable crank that served as an accelerator to the trolley's other end and drove off.

ST. PETERSBURG'S PLEASURE PALACE, the original Million Dollar Pier building. At its opening in 1926, an estimated 3,000 couples danced on the rooftop's open-air ballroom. It was later roofed over because night humidity made the dance floor too slippery.

ST. PETERSBURG TO HAVANA boat race, shown near the starting line in the 1930s, was an annual highly publicized event before the Castro regime in Cuba. After its demise, a major international yachting event, the Southern Ocean race, was launched each year from the downtown waterfront. Since World War II, yachting has become a major activity in St. Petersburg, abetted in part by the city's most famous yachtsman, Charley Morgan. His Morgan Yacht Corp. manufactured widely popular sailing craft between 22 and 56 feet in length. In the summer of 1970 he built and captained the *Heritage* for the 12-meter American Cup races at Newport RI.

TWO HISTORIC SCHOOL BUILDINGS remained part of downtown for decades until giving way to government offices. In foreground at left is the Graded School, St. Petersburg's first school built with a $7,000 bond issue in 1893. It was at the corner of Fifth Street North and Second Avenue. To its right in center is the Manual Training School, built by E. H. Tomlinson in 1901. It later became an annex for an adjacent City Hall. The photo is looking northeast. Church spire at upper right marks St. Peter's Episcopal Church on Fourth Street North, built in 1899.

SMALL FLYING FIELD along the waterfront south of Central Avenue in 1929 was named Whitted Field after the St. Petersburg aviator Albert Whitted, who served as a flying instructor during World War I and was killed in a plane crash near Pensacola in 1923. The field in the 1930s also housed a hangar for Goodyear blimps *(top right)* that began flying out of St. Petersburg in 1929. Whitted Field also was the birthplace in 1934 of National Airlines.

WEST COAST INN on First Street South in the 1930s, across from Al Lang Field. It had none of the elegance of the Vinoy Park Hotel, yet it was owned by the same Laughner Enterprises. One thing the inn did have was character. Many of its tenants were health addicts and chose the inn because it was situated across the street from the Fountain of Youth with its supposedly curative sulphur waters. Because of its proximity to Al Lang Field, numerous Major League baseball players also took rooms at the inn. A story that gained credence through repetition was that Babe Ruth once drove a home run so far out of Al Lang Field that it crashed through a window at the West Coast Inn, and tenants, as a memorial, left the jagged window in place until the inn was demolished in 1967.

SIREN'S SONG

Druggist James Earl "Doc" Webb reached St. Petersburg in 1925 with $5,000 and a flair for business. His first store, nested between two sets of railway tracks, was so keenly run that by 1937 sales dollars were counted in the millions. By the 1950s Doc's Webb's City was an institution, beloved for low prices and high quality.

From a three-cent full breakfast (later upped to 14 cents) to a grocery brimming with fresh produce, to fashion outlets featuring brand names, Webb's City eventually occupied seven city blocks with 76 stores that drew 60,000 daily customers. Prescriptions were filled, checks were cashed, cars were repaired, and diners were fed. Webb's gas station pumped the south's highest volume of fuel for three cents less than anyone else; his fountain sated 12,000 appetites each day; his 40-chair barbershop scissored through two shifts of barbers; his ice cream plant oozed 1,000 gallons daily of the creamy treat.

Gigantic as it was, Webb's City remained a neighborly meeting place, virtually the city's only shopping outlet patronized equally by black and white customers. Everyone seemed acquainted, and "Doc" was usually there to personally greet his customers.

Adding to that aura of familiarity was the fourth-floor "talking mermaid" show. Visitors would peek into the sirens' cave through ship portholes. Before them lolled fish-tailed mannequin mermaids, scantily clad in well-placed sea fans and costume jewelry.

Swiping a page from the Wizard of Oz, Webb had secreted a sultry-voiced, microphoned woman behind the scene. "That's a mighty nice hat you're wearing," she would coo to a startled viewer. Or, after receiving a note slipped by a visitor's friend, she would welcome the person by name, inviting him or her to come back sometime to take a swim. It was a testimony to those simpler times that viewers seemed genuinely delighted to converse with mannequins.

But sophistication inevitably overtakes simple pleasures. By the mid-1960s, Webb's City increasingly became a victim of suburban sprawl and of the declining vigor of Webb and the downtown area. Discount franchises were chipping away at his customer base.

More serious, perhaps, was that consumer tastes had changed.

What once had been regarded as a whimsically innocent novelty, Webb's City was increasingly regarded as a bastion of tastelessness frequented only by the poor and elderly. Tourists crossed Webb's City off their destination lists.

Animal rights activists charged that Webb's "dancing" chickens were actually hopping around to avoid a hotfoot. The mermaid display was revamped with skimpier costumes and the addition of a pair of presumably amorous sailor mannequins. The souvenir shop grew fat with coconut shell monkey faces, stuffed alligators, and conch shell crucifixes.

Not even Webb's motto of "stack it high and sell it cheap" was capable of saving his sinking city. In 1974, following his wife's death, the 75-year-old Webb retired. A Texas businessman kept "the store of tomorrow" open five more years. One hot August day in 1979, after 54 years, the World's Most Unusual Drugstore quietly slipped into St. Petersburg history.

TWO BASEBALL GREATS at Al Lang Field in 1934. Lou Gehrig (*left*) and Babe Ruth in one of their last photos as both members of the New York Yankees (the fan with them is Dick Mayes). The following year Ruth played for the Boston Braves. The Yankees held Spring training in St. Petersburg from 1925 through 1961. For Major League baseball, St. Petersburg has been the nation's premier Spring training city. First to come to town were the St. Louis Browns, in 1914. Most years the city often has had two Major League teams training simultaneously during the Spring.

FLORIDA THEATER, the city's grandest movie house, opened in 1926 on the east side of Fifth Street South between Central and First avenues. This photo, taken in 1936, spells out the feature film on the marquee as *After The Thin Man* starring William Powell and Myrna Loy. On facing page *(top)* are box seats. They contained no seats but, instead, behind the draperies, the pipes for the massive organ in the theater pit. Opulent furnishings on facing page *(bottom)* decorated the lobby. The 2,300-seat theater was demolished in 1967 for a bank parking lot.

115

WSUN RADIO STUDIOS were on the Million Dollar Pier when the station opened in 1927. It was operated by the Chamber of Commerce but when the expense got too great the city took it over. In 1953, it added WSUN-TV, Channel 38, the first television station on Florida's west coast. Both were sold in the 1960s. The studios *(above)* were on the second floor of a wing of the Million Dollar Pier. The wing faced west, toward downtown. A trolley bringing passengers to the pier entered the ground floor and turned around for the trip back to town.

THE BEE LINE FERRY made eight roundtrips daily from the southern tip of Pinellas County across Tampa Bay to Manatee County, a 45-minute ride. Before the Sunshine Skyway, a southern-bound traveler had a choice — take the ferry or drive across Gandy Bridge and through Tampa to get to the Bradenton/Sarasota area. The ferry began operating in 1926. Nothing fancy, the tugboat-like vessels reduced the mileage to Bradenton by 43 miles from the overland Tampa route. Talk about building a bridge or a tunnel across lower Tampa Bay was plentiful for decades but not until 1939 was a port authority formed to get on with the job. Plans were interrupted by World War II but the famous Sunshine Skyway bridge finally was in place between Pinellas and Manatee counties in 1954. When it opened, the Bee Line Ferry closed.

FAVORITE MEETING SITE of the many state Tourist Societies in St. Petersburg was the Million Dollar Pier building. This state group in a night meeting on the ground floor in the 1930s most likely was planning its next social, for the societies enjoyed regular get-togethers to talk about what cities they were from. After the building was demolished in 1967, the societies had mostly dissipated but those that survived found the new pier building less suitable for their meetings. The original building, with its openness, catered to group activities: the replacement building was designed to make money and thus used much of its interior space for gift shops and other commercial enterprises.

CHRISTMAS IN ST. PETERSBURG in 1939, and for many years thereafter, meant creation of Christmas Tree Lane, the lighting of scores of Australian pine trees that lined both sides of the Municipal Pier. The Yuletide spirit also prompted the trolley conductors to dress as Santa Claus and to decorate their cars.

GETTING ACQUAINTED ON THE FAMOUS GREEN BENCHES was the title of this post card showing Central Avenue in the 1930s. Because the benches were associated with elderly people, St. Petersburg took a beating in the media. A 1958 *Holiday* magazine stated, "The old people sit, passengers in a motionless streetcar without destination." An estimated 3,000 benches lined downtown streets during their greatest popularity between the 1920s and 1970s. To soften the negative image, the Suncoast Advertising Club in 1961 got official sanction to repaint the benches in pastel colors. A year later the City Council, under pressure from older citizens to bring back the green, and noting the unsightly peeling of the new pastels, permitted a return to the original color.

TREASURE ISLAND CAUSEWAY nearing completion in 1939 between Boca Ciega Bay and the Gulf of Mexico. Leading to the largely undeveloped beaches, the causeway was preceded by two other bridges to the Gulf beaches — one was the McAdoo Bridge from Fifth Avenue South, the other the Welch Causeway west of Pinellas Park. At left in foreground is the Sunset Hotel. At the western end of Central Avenue, the Sunset was the only hotel not within walking distance of downtown when it was built in 1915.

NOT ENDORSED by all but used to lure tourists were photos sent North of bathing-suit clad young ladies in odd recreational pursuits. Such skin pics, plus Webb's City promotions depicting young girls in bubble baths, along with pitches by the city's Solarium to come tan in the buff, upset Puritan minds in town. Many citizens were especially scandalized when fan-dancer Sally Rand was strutted out onto Spa Beach for a tantalizing publicity shot. All this "shameless" promotion took place only a few decades after the city refused to appropriate $500 to promote tourism, calling the expenditure too "frivolous."

ANCHORED IN THE MIDDLE of Sixth Street just north of Central Avenue were a pair of streetcars that served as the core of the city's trolley system. All streetcars touched base here to begin their runs, transfer passengers, and end their trips. In 1936 the city began converting from streetcars to buses, and in 1944 tore down the Sixth Street transit base. Five years later the last streetcar made its final run in St. Petersburg. The new transit system's headquarters for catching a bus or transferring became a small permanent building built on the south side of Williams Park. In a nostalgic mood during the 1960s, the city considered a return to the picturesque streetcars sans rails, but officials chose to continue with its diesel-fumed buses.

WORLD WAR II RECRUITS flooded into St. Petersburg beginning in mid-1942 for six weeks of basic training. They filled the city's hotels and rooming houses and overflowed into camps called "Tent City." The largest camp was some 10,000 recruits in the Jungle area of west St. Petersburg. Initial military headquarters in town was the Vinoy Park Hotel. By August 1943, all military personnel had moved on, mostly to overseas assignments.

FEW U.S. ARMY SOLDIERS began their wartime service in more favorable
surroundings. They got their instruction under huge banyan trees along the waterfront
in one of the nation's balmiest climates. Many bunked in the city's most luxurious
hotels and took their meals in downtown cafeterias. The post-war boom in St. Petersburg
often is traced in part to servicemen who, remembering the beauty of the Sunshine
City, moved their families here in the 1950s.

CHAMBER OF COMMERCE
presents
"MELODY CRUISE"

An Outdoor MUSICAL REVUE and AQUACADE
Round Lake Park, March 28, 29, 1940   Nightly at 8:00
Staged and Directed by LOYD SPANGLER

ROUND LAKE, a small tranquil body of water west of Fourth Street North near Seventh Avenue, for decades was the site of the annual Festival of States pageantry. The above is from the program for the 22nd annual event, held in March of 1940. On a lakeshore stage the sponsoring Chamber of Commerce produced musical spectacles and water exhibitions in which the swimmers wore suits that glowed in the dark.

BARGAIN GROCERIES AT WEBB'S CITY, and low prices throughout "Doc" Webb's complex, cut into sales of other merchants throughout the city. Nevertheless, competitors admired Webb's promotional genius. For years Webb negotiated a tough advertising contract with the *Times* ensuring he would always have a double-page space reserved for his ads in the newspaper's A section. On rare occasions of historic news, when the *Times* needed the entire A section for reporting events, Webb would not waive his contract for the occasion. So readers would find among the cataclysmic events of the day the usual two pages of Webb's City specials.

CRUISING INTO DOWNTOWN from the Big Bayou area in the 1940s is this streetcar approaching Central Avenue along Fifth Street South. All streetcars started and departed from Central Transfer Station at Central Avenue and Sixth Street. Fares were 10 cents until 6:30 p.m., 5 cents in the evening, or 15-ride tickets for $1. Large white building at right is the rear of the La Plaza Theater. The Florida Power Corp. in background was the firm's headquarters from 1925 until 1972, when it moved its main offices to 34th Street South.

BAY PINES VETERANS HOSPITAL was one of the few federal projects St. Petersburg acquired from the Hoover Administration in Washington, D.C. Learning in 1931 that the Veterans Administration was planning a major veterans hospital in Florida, two state legislators from the St. Petersburg area pressured the VA to pick St. Petersburg. The VA insisted the land must be donated. Offered was acreage along Boca Ciega Bay. The VA agreed to the site in 1931 and by 1933 the Bay Pines hospital (*above*), and an accompanying VA regional center, were dedicated.

GORGEOUS GORGES

Fine dining has always been one of the pleasures of living in St. Petersburg. Some of the city's best known restaurants offered ambience that was as attractive as the food they served. But many, despite brisk business, are gone.

Rollande et Pierre's on Fourth Street North was especially charming. Not known to be a casual "drop-in for dinner" establishment, reservations were always needed at the small French country house. Patrons often dined there to celebrate special occasions. It was cozy, candlelit, and fragrant — no place for piped-in elevator music — so serenades were provided by a strolling violinist. The menu, of course, included escargot, an order of which often quieted the entire dining room as everyone paused to watch their fellow diner pull the first buttery snail from its shell.

Upscale, too, but considerably more spacious was the Sand Dollar on 34th Street South. Tourists and residents alike enjoyed the orange glazed duck or the tender prime rib. While awaiting a table, guests would stroll the gift shop that specialized in jewelry made of sand dollars, or take cocktails at the sizeable circular and revolving bar just off the dining room.

One downtown favorite was the Chatterbox. A hint of Manhattan at Beach Drive and Central Avenue, this Art Deco-style steak house was tucked under an immense banyan tree. It was torn down for construction of the Bayfront Towers, a swap that many citizens tried to prevent not simply out of fondness for the Chatterbox, but because the century-old banyan would be destroyed.

Perhaps no restaurant compared to the Wedgewood Inn across from Bartlett Park. Whenever visiting friends or relatives arrived, the Wedgewood was a must on the itinerary. Not only was the restaurant canopied by huge trees and built alongside a creek but its dining room was shrouded in exotic flowering plants and trees. One of the shady, glassed dining rooms even featured an aviary of colorful birds. It took only one slice to forever recall the Wedgewood's "World Most Famous" apple pie. And a la mode? To die for.

Less exotic but wildly popular was Aunt Hattie's, across from Albert Whitted Field. Patrons could expect to be handed a number at the door with seating sometimes taking an hour. The delay never deterred customers, for the restaurant was a veritable museum full of antique treasures. The homestyle menu (a favorite was gravied meatloaf) and the comfortable latticed booths were especially favored by older, retired guests.

If a night on the town began at one of the upscale restaurants, it often ended in the wee hours at one of two less auspicious eateries. Tuxedoed gents and their begowned ladies — even entire parties of Coliseum revelers not quite ready to end the fun — usually stopped off at The Owl Diner on Fourth Street North, or at Wolfie's at Central Plaza.

The Owl's platters of eggs, bacon, potatoes, or grits were ever-ready. Over many years, loving regulars had filled every nook of the restaurant with gift owls of every conceivable size and shape. Diners at Wolfie's adored the New York atmosphere and feasted on hot pastrami or a Mogambo Extravaganza dessert deluged in whipped cream.

All are now gone — indelible only in memories of evenings when people dressed for dinner.

SPA POOL on the north side of the Municipal Pier in the 1940s. Built in 1913, Spa Pool featured a heated indoor freshwater pool, plus medicinal baths and massages. The pool was a favorite of St. Petersburg youngsters. Admission in the 1940s was 35 cents plus 5 cents for a towel. Adjoining it on the west was the Solarium, where adults could sunbathe in the nude, also for an admission fee of 35 cents. Both buildings provided access to the outdoor Spa Beach. They were demolished in the early 1960s.

THE NORTH MOLE has had a variety of uses over the decades. It is the spit of land on the north side of Municipal Pier. Here in the 1940s it is the site for a city marina and for the Spa Pool and Solarium. Earlier it served as an air terminal for airboat aviator Tony Jannus. Albert Whitted also had a hangar for his planes on the mole. Couples danced the nights away at the Green Lantern next to Whitted's hangar, and the city's Historic Museum has had a presence on the site since 1922. Its counterpart, South Mole, has become Demens' Landing.

ACL RAILROAD DEPOT in the 1940s was in the heart of downtown, at First Avenue South between Second and Third streets. Built in 1915 on the site of the city's original depot, the Orange Belt Railway, the ACL structure was pressured out of the downtown in 1963 because the railroad tracks running down the center of First Avenue South were both an unpleasing sight and a hindrance to increasing auto traffic. The depot relocated in west St. Petersburg on 31st Street North.

VINTAGE 1945 was to some oldtimers the last decade that downtown and the charming and spacious waterfront were leisurely pleasant. Slips in the yacht basin were easy to come by. The South Mole was undeveloped except for the Junior Yacht Club where many youngsters took sailing lessons in prams. Municipal Pier still sported the Spa Pool and dozens of Australian pines up and down its length. The massive Bayfront Center with its acres of asphalt parking had not yet intruded on the symmetrical park, with its oft-frequented Fountain of Youth, just south of Al Lang Field. Aged banyan trees still rooted where Bayfront Towers would eventually block sunsets. And a baseball fan could watch a Spring training ballgame at Al Lang Field from his room in the West Coast Inn, a building later razed for an impersonal chain hotel. Much of this serenity in the late 1940s and early 1950s ended with the beginning of an economic boom.

THE FINEST IN THE SOUTH, said educators of St. Petersburg High School when it opened in 1926. Accolades included "unique architecture...enormous auditorium with a stage as large as those in the greatest theaters...shower rooms...individual lockers...cafeteria for 1,200...private waterworks and electric plant...tennis courts, baseball diamonds, football gridiron." Principal from its opening and for the next 21 years was Albert J. Geiger. In 1926, it was the city's only high school. The following year Gibbs High School was built.

RAH! RAH! RAH! Students and their leaders in 1941 *(right)* were a wholesome looking lot, and chose as their school motto "Loyalty and Service to God, Country, and Home." Noted for outstanding sports teams, St. Petersburg High gridders *(below)* took to the field in the latest protective leather pads and helmets and the starting 11 played both offense and defense. A season was successful only if the Green Devils defeated a chief rival, the Terriers of Hillsborough High School.

CROWDED CENTRAL AVENUE, between Fourth and Fifth streets, after the War.

NO RESTAURANT had the variety of clientele as the Owl. Open around the clock, it attracted the hungry from every economic strata. Drop in for breakfast and your companion at the counter could be a streetcar conductor or a stockbroker, a hotel bellhop or a bank president, a musician or a mortician, a vagrant or a veterinarian. All would casually ogle the ceiling-high shelves of thousands of owl knickknacks. The Owl Diner is first remembered as being at Fourth Street South and First Avenue, then moving to Fourth Street North between Second and Third avenues (*above*). It later abandoned the diner motif and built an attractive brick restaurant on the site.

SCENE OF AN ENVIRONMENTAL BATTLE, one of the city's first, occurred around this inauspicious restaurant on Beach Drive near Central Avenue. The Art Deco-styled Chatterbox was an attractive dinner scene for decades but before entering, customers often paused to marvel at the adjacent giant banyan tree. Thousands of charcoal-broiled steaks later, in the early 1970s, the Chatterbox block was chosen to be the site of the Bayfront Towers. Protests erupted, not so much for the Chatterbox's fate but for the proposed destruction of the banyan tree. Eventually, developers won.

GANDY'S WHITE ELEPHANT, it was called, until it proved itself a favorite with the public. It was the La Plaza Theater. The theater auditorium (*above*) occupied the northwest corner of First Avenue South and Fifth Street, but the entrance was a patio walk (*right*) that fronted on Central Avenue. The La Plaza opened in March 1913 with a performance of an opera by the Royal Italian Company. Condemned in 1953, the theater was demolished in 1957.

THE ONLY SHOW IN TOWN

By the mid-1950s about one-fourth of St. Petersburg homes were illumed by television's silvery halo. Residents each evening doused the lights, aligned chairs theater-fashion in their living rooms, popped a pan of greasy popcorn, and settled in to view the only show in town: WSUN-TV — Channel 38.

The station's smiling Mr. Sun test pattern at first glowed dimly and fuzzily in 1953 when broadcasts began at the former trolley turn-around of the Million Dollar Pier. City-owned and manned by former radio engineers, WSUN's broadcasts were a creative mix of local talent, early live remotes, music, movies, sporting events, and cartoons.

Local news, sports, and weather celebrities included Jack Swift and Guy Bagley. Harry Smith and Charlotte Joh were popular hosts of a video juke box — early music videos — on which filmed musical numbers featured stars like Gail Storm and Guy Mitchell. Webb's Television Theater provided movie fare.

Despite bulky cameras, WSUN aired the area's earliest live remotes, including the Festival of States parade. But local live television's true star was beamed from a Clearwater auction house, where vibrant, flower-shirted Howard the Trader beckoned a live audience and viewers to "Talk to this ol' boy" — to bid on merchandise from antiques to zippers. Once bids ended, the home audience could also order those items via mail at the bid price. The earliest known "home shopping," Howard's program was wildly popular, and Tampa Bay area families trooped by the scores to Howard's Clearwater auction house.

Live in the pier studio was a country variety "Home Show," which featured Daisy May and Ol' Brother Charley, who showed off big-name Nashville stars like Little Jimmy Dickens. One slim local teen named Bobby Lord became so popular that he went on to Nashville.

WSUN became an ABC affiliate about 1955 and programs flourished. Soon, everyone laughed at Betty White in Life with Elizabeth, and Our Miss Brooks with Eve Arden.

Perhaps no St. Petersburg TV audience was as attentive as the children. Parents reported that their kids watched even the WSUN test pattern. Then the station paraded a programing dummy-whammy every afternoon: the Mickey Mouse Club followed by local star, Burl McCarty, who portrayed "Captain Mac."

The pith-helmeted captain, adorned in a colorful patterned shirt, each weekday welcomed St. Pete youngsters to the pier studio. There, children not only appeared on camera (thus briefly becoming school celebrities) but sat raptly viewing Ramar of the Jungle serials and Crusader Rabbit cartoons, with the Captain himself.

Teen viewers were invited on Saturday morning's Teen Time Jamboree, a locally produced sock hop.

Predictably, WSUN soon was followed on air by other Tampa Bay broadcasters, first WFLA and WTVT then WLCY. They raided Channel 38's talent pool, including songster Ernie Lee and June Hurley (later to be Romper Room's "Miss June").

By 1960, its ABC affiliateship lost, WSUN ownership passed to private hands and failing, fell dark.

EARLY WSUN-TV STAR was Burl McCarty who, as the character Captain Mac, was a big hit with St. Petersburg's children.

MOST POPULAR WSUN-TV program for adults featured the dynamic Clearwater auctioneer, Howard K. Ewing, better known as "Howard the Trader." He sold a variety of merchandise at bargain prices to his auction house audience and to TV viewers.

STRETCHING 15 miles across Tampa Bay, connecting Pinellas County to Manatee County, the initial Sunshine Skyway was a single span bridge finished in 1954 and carrying a $1.75 toll. Vertical clearance was 150 feet, highest in the state. For some motorists, the elevation was too scary and they avoided it but traffic became so heavy that a twin span was added in 1971.

THE LAST DEPOT DOWNTOWN was this double-story passenger station of the Atlantic Coast Line Railroad along First Avenue South near Second Street. The photo, taken in the late 1950s, is looking west from a bricked alley just south of Central Avenue. Building in background is the Bainbridge Hotel. Within several years, the depot was closed when the ACL was asked to move out of the downtown and remove its tracks from the center of First Avenue South.

A FORLORN FIGURE strolls down the sidewalk in a rare scene — a nearly abandoned Million Dollar Pier. Taken at the end of the 1950s, the photo almost portends the oncoming fate of the recreational building at the pier's end. Soon city leaders would persuade the public that the building, nearly 35 years old at this time, was in too much disrepair to be renovated. Attendance at the building did taper off in the 1950s, due in part to the placing of parking meters along the pier. Many residents and fishermen complained about the end of free pier parking.

THE CORNERSTONE of Central Plaza just south of Central Avenue at 34th Street was the serving-at-all-hours Wolfie's Restaurant. No restaurant in town surpassed Wolfie's in pastrami sandwiches or ice cream desserts. Central Plaza was one of St. Petersburg's first shopping malls. It opened in 1952 on acreage formerly known as Goose Pond, a wetland. Stores in the plaza included William Henry and Belk-Lindsey department stores, Publix, Saltz Shoes, McCrory's dimestore, and more than a dozen small shops. At the time, Central Plaza was an innovative shopping experience because of the variety of stores and plentiful free parking but its business quickly suffered when giant shopping complexes like Tyrone Mall were built.

NO UPHOLSTERED CHAIRS, private booths, or subtle lighting but still the ambience at the Wedgewood Inn was an experience in dining. Success of the nearly all-wood and glass dinner spot across from Bartlett Park was attributed to, besides its excellent food, the tropical motif. Tourists, and out-of-state guests of residents, were enchanted by the lush greenery surrounding the tables, and the music — not an orchestra or piped-in elevator music but the melodious songs emanating from an giant aviary of exotic birds that shared the dining room with patrons.

UNPLANNED DEVELOPMENT of First Avenue South near the waterfront resulted in the site becoming a congested transportation hub. This photo in the late 1950s looking west on the avenue highlights problem. The Greyhound Lines bus depot in foreground funneled its buses out onto the avenue. At the same time, passenger trains of the Atlantic Coast Line Railroad, using tracks down the center of First Avenue, deposited its riders at its depot (at right, under trees). Meanwhile, traffic-attracting businesses also clustered around the avenue — on the left the Lincoln-Mercury car dealer, Goodwill Industries, the Gotham Hotel, the Seneca Hotel, *The Times*, The *Evening Independent*, and to the right the Florida Theater, and the Bainbridge Hotel. A decade later, half of the structures, along with the railroad tracks, had been removed.

A SIMPLER TIME

St. Petersburg, in the 1950s, was a city designed for the enjoyment of its people. On a typical summer Saturday, families often mapped out an itinerary that brought parents and children downtown for shopping, for entertainment, for dining, and just to enjoy other people.

For a few dimes, the family could catch an early morning bus whose destination sign read Webb's City. Dad headed straight for the barbershop — an eight-minute cut cost two bits. His wife wandered off to buy linens or leaf through the dress racks to admire the latest fashions. The children were on their own, climbing the stairs to go watch the mermaid show and the dancing chickens. An hour later, all would meet downstairs for a cone of two baseball-sized scoops of ice cream. Five cents each.

It was just a three-block walk to the Florida Theater, where family films regularly played. Once the kids were inside the air-conditioned movie palace, Mom and Dad walked the half block to Central Avenue, where green benches already were filling and the sidewalks flowing with well-dressed people.

No one came downtown half-dressed. Women wore fresh frocks, men kept on suit coats and ties, with the occasional boutonniere, available from Webb's City for a dime. Most parents did not permit their children to appear in public in shorts or tennis shoes.

Dad might grab an empty seat on a back-to-back bench. While watching the promenade of shoppers, he likely struck up a conversation with the gent next to him. They may have talked about how a military man like Ike was doing as president or about the trolley tracks being removed from Central Avenue now that buses had replaced the old streetcars.

Meanwhile, his wife weaved in an out of Woolworths, Kress's, McCrory's, Walgreens's, all in the same block, and might have ventured down the street to the town's leading department store, Willson-Chase.

At a prearranged time, the family gathered in Simpson's restaurant for lunch. Sometimes Dad opted out, preferring to go nearby to the Jockey Club where they would draw him a cold draft to go along with the bar's famous juicy hamburgers.

The next stop — the Municipal Pier — was a bit of a jaunt of six blocks but the kids were up to it. Mom dug two bathing suits out of her purse, gave each child 35 cents for admission to Spa Pool, and the parents watched them race down the street. If they didn't part company, the family could browse the cool shops inside the pier, where a favorite children's purchase was a tiny pet turtle.

Ready to call it a day, the family headed toward Williams Park for a bus home. Passing the Soreno, they likely would see a small crowd of starchly dressed young people being escorted by their parents to that evening's cotillion.

At Williams Park, the family lingered for one last pleasure. Dad escorted his family to a park bench. There they rested at the band shell to watch and listen to the Sunshine City Band playing a selection rousing Sousa marches. All on a summer Saturday in the 1950s.

LIGHTING UP THE SKY in 1942 for blocks around Ninth Street South were the many stores in the Webb's City mercantile complex. Many nights towering spinning ferris wheels and carnival rides brought in by "Doc" Webb also lit up the horizon, beckoning shoppers from miles around.

FLYING INTO ST. PETERSBURG from the south over the Sunshine Skyway bridge emphasizes the city's intensive development around the water. To the right of 34th Street in center of this circa 1960 photo is the Pinellas Point area with Lake Maggiore and the downtown above it. At upper right is a new Howard Frankland bridge across Tampa Bay. Finger fills at left, shaped to provide canals and therefore waterfront residential sites, began cluttering Boca Ciega Bay. The Bayway connecting the mainland to Tierra Verde and the islands leading to Fort De Soto was still in the planning stage.

ALL ABOARD FOR THE LAST TRAIN. Exactly 75 years elapsed from the day in 1888 when the first railroad, the Orange Belt, deposited passengers downtown to the day the last passenger train, the Atlantic Coast Line, pulled out. A crowd gathered in front of the ACL train and station in 1963 for the final departure. As St. Petersburg's downtown grew, the First Avenue South site of the ACL proved too disruptive to both pedestrian and auto traffic. So ACL left the scene, its depot to be razed and its tracks removed from the center of the avenue. Behind train is the old Harrison Hardware & Furniture building, later Easton's, and to its right is the corner Stag Hotel.

FORT DE SOTO PARK in the 1960s prior to its connection to the mainland via the Bayway. A county park, and one of the nation's finest, it comprises five islands – Madelaine Key, St. Jean Key, St. Christopher Key, Bonne Fortune Key, and the main island, Mullet Key. Together, they total 900 acres with seven miles of waterfront. Mullet Key gained its significance as a stopover for explorer Ponce de Leon, and as the site of a garrison of Union soldiers during the Civil War. Construction of the still-existing fort began in 1898. During World War I it was activated as a Coast Artillery Training Center, and in World War II was used as an Air Corps gunnery and bombing training center. Pinellas County purchased Mullet Key, except for Fort De Soto, in 1938. Ten years later the county acquired also the fort and numerous surrounding islands, the U.S. Government stipulating all be used solely as a park and for recreational purposes. The road to the park was completed in 1963.

AN ISLAND OF MANY DREAMS, Weedon Island remains an undeveloped jewel in northeast St. Petersburg. The 1,000-acre peninsula, with its five miles of beaches, in 1972 was placed on the National Register of Historic Places. It was home to native Indian tribes, was explored by Hernando de Soto, and is a significant archaeological site. Named for Dr. Leslie W. Weedon, who in 1898 moved to the heavily wooded peninsula, large tracts of it sold repeatedly, each owner announcing grand plans to capitalize on the site's beauty. It once housed a nightclub, an airport, a movie studio. Plans once were drawn to build an upscale subdivision, as well as a mammoth floral garden. But wars and the Depression thwarted them all. Nearly all the peninsula was bought by the state in 1973 for $6-million. The only major construction on Weedon Island has been the Florida Power Corp. power plant.

ONCE A FISHING VILLAGE, as all coastal Florida towns were in the 19th Century, St. Petersburg learned quickly its future and fortune was in tourism, not tarpon. Catches in the Gulf of Mexico still were plentiful in the 1960s (*above*) but dredge and fill, waterfront development, pollution, and overfishing were soon to dwindle a day's harvest with the nets.

THE BAYWAY, for St. Petersburg residents, was as much of an achievement and necessity as the building of Gandy Bridge and the Sunshine Skyway. The latter two provided access to Hillsborough and Manatee counties, but the Bayway gave residents of the beaches and islands to the west and south of St. Petersburg a quick and travel-saving route into downtown. Shown under construction in the early 1960s (*above*), the Bayway included 15 miles of causeways and bridges. The photo is looking westward with St. Petersburg Beach at top. Property at left of thoroughfare, which is 54th Avenue South, is under development as Florida Presbyterian College (later renamed Eckerd College).

LAWN BOWLING in the 1960s at the Mirror Lake complex for senior citizens began when a club was organized for the sport in 1916. Its adherents often were also members of the city's shuffleboard club, whose participants competed on adjacent courts. Visitors to the Mirror Lake area also could watch roque, chess, and horseshoe pitching competitions. For many, the sunny, quiet complex was an oasis of low-key pleasure, not only for transplants from northern states but for large numbers of Canadians, who wintered in St. Petersburg and are shown competing under their own flag.

AN OUTSTANDING YEAR for St. Petersburg's venture into bigtime art and entertainment was 1965. That year the city dedicated two major waterfront structures, the Museum of Fine Arts on Beach Drive and the Bayfront Center just south of Al Lang Field. Posing for a lighted portrait after its dedication *(above)*, the Bayfront with its auditorium and theater proved invaluable. It attracted symphony orchestras, professional sports, touring Broadway shows, conventions, the "Greatest Show on Earth," and scores of events that used to bypass St. Petersburg for lack of a suitable performing site. Before the Bayfront, visiting entertainment had to settle for the Coliseum or the National Guard Armory, sometimes even the floor space at the Gay Blades Roller Rink.

157

THE NEWSROOM

Most major daily newspapers have their characters, particularly in the newsroom. The *St. Petersburg Times*, even during its summit years of the 1960s and 1970s, did not. Instead, it had personalities. The *Times* was too patriarchal, too much the image of owner Nelson Poynter, to employ eccentrics. NP, as he signed his memos, often ventured into the newsroom, but he knew few of his news staffers by name. His visits were made not to mix or greet reporters and editors but usually to seek out a staff member to convey a thought or criticism. To many staffers, his wife Henrietta, despite her long-strutting steps and postured aloofness, was the more sociable, more approachable.

In this somewhat straightjacket environment the *Times* still produced many memorable people. Among them was Tom Harris, who came to work in a blue suit that by noon was grey from cigar ashes. He ran the newsroom and he lived in it. Once the paper had gone to press and the newsroom was empty, Harris often searched for a lingering soul to accompany him to Wolfie's at Central Plaza for a midnight snack and more shop talk.

Harris enjoyed shocking cub reporters and interns while acquainting them with the copy desk. He would grab a canister of rubber cement, used to paste copy together, and brush it up and down his suit trousers. Before the shock wore off the young faces, the glue had dried and Harris rubbed it off with his hand, the trousers none the worse.

He never accepted the urging of columnist Dick Bothwell to trade in the cigar for a bag of horehound candies. A non-smoker, Bothwell kept the candy on his desk for anyone trying to end the nicotine habit. He was a popular luncheon speaker, delivering humorous speeches while sketching caricatures on an easel.

Many *Times* editors declined invitations to speak to clubs. The newspaper has never been considered to be the "popular press" in St. Petersburg, often because of its strong editorial positions. As a result, *Times*' luncheon speakers, once the plates were cleared, frequently were assailed with offensive questions.

Among those reluctant to appear at such functions was Don Baldwin, the editor who guided the newspaper to its 1964 Pulitzer Prize for Public Service. Expert at developing a staff and getting the most from it, Baldwin finished his workdays on time and seldom hung around the newsroom or frequented cocktail parties. He preferred relaxing at home with his classical guitar.

Under Baldwin, the *Times* became the bay area's dominant newspaper; Baldwin routinely raided the *Tampa Tribune's* newsroom of its best talent. He practically hired away the Trib's front page — reporters Martin Waldron, Don Meiklejohn, and Jack Nease. Soon the *Times* was outselling the *Tribune*,.

Eventually, all left the *Times*, including Baldwin. Some moved their bylines to more national newspapers, some retired, and others lost interest in newspapering once newsrooms were carpeted, as occurred at the *Times*. Unfortunately, as cigarette butts on the floor, phone numbers scribbled on the walls, and desks cluttered with stained cups of curdled coffee from the previous night disappeared, so did the characters and personalities of the newsroom, at the *Times* and at many newspapers.

HOME OF THE ST. PETERSBURG *INDEPENDENT*, the southwest corner of First Avenue South and Fifth Street. Started in 1906 as a weekly, it became a daily in 1907 and changed its name to the *Evening Independent*. As Florida morning newspapers flourished, including the *Times*, and afternoon papers lost circulation, the Thomson newspaper chain offered to sell the *Evening Independent* to the *Times*. Nelson Poynter, owner of the *Times*, paid $300,000 for the failing afternoon paper whose circulation had dwindled to 19,000. The *Times* demolished the *Independent* building but continued publishing the afternoon newspaper until 1986, then closed it down.

THE VISION AND WISDOM of city leaders as far back as 1905, when waterfront land was purchased for the city as a future park, is evident in this late 1960s photo taken from atop the Vinoy Park Hotel toward the south. Few cities in the nation present their citizens with such a beautiful and valuable vista. Viewers will recognize the newly completed Museum of Fine Arts at right and the Bayfront Center in the distance.

VALUABLE VACANT REAL ESTATE in the late 1960s frustrated city leaders who were trying to package a multimillion dollar commercial project that would include a major hotel. A site for it had already been cleared (*left center*), just south of the new Federal Building on First Avenue South, completed in 1967. The city had also rearranged the small park south of Al Lang Field to provide a requested infield practice diamond for the St. Louis Cardinals. In doing so, it chose to save the nearly century-old Fountain of Youth on the park's west side.

FOR ITS TIME, the twin-span Sunshine Skyway was an eye-catching engineering feat. And it was expected to last into the 21st Century. But because of heavy traffic and a horrendous ship tragedy, the state chose to demolish both spans for a still higher and wider bridge. The Skyway's initial span was opened in 1954, followed by construction of the second span in 1971. Nine years later, a freighter struck the pilings of one of the spans, dumping a Greyhound bus and several automobiles into Tampa Bay 150 feet below. Killed were 35 people. Work began soon after on a new bridge with emphasis on safety pylons that would protect bridge pilings from another wayward ship disaster.

FOR A WILLIAMS PARK CROWD a high school band from New Jersey plays an afternoon concert during a 1960s Festival of States celebration. Each of the 20-some out-of-state high school bands that competed in the various Festival parades always scheduled a free concert in the park for the people of St. Petersburg, in appreciation of the city's hospitality. The bands began playing at 10 a.m. and would continue into the evening hours.

LANDMARK DRIVE-IN and one of the first in town was the Barrel, a neon-glowing curb service restaurant at 16th Street and First Avenue South. Its pink glowing pig atop the round building was a beacon for both families and teenagers wishing a hamburger and frosted root beer. Often crowded with cars, the Barrel lost some of its appeal during the 1960s when the civil rights movement resulted in racial disturbances in the parking lot.

DOWNTOWN ST. PETERSBURG IN late 1970. New pyramidal pier building is under construction at end of pier, the John Knox Apartments have just been completed (tall structure in foreground), and most of the government buildings around City Hall on the southeast side of Mirror Lake are in operation. St. Petersburg population in 1970 hit 216,232 and its black citizens for the first time gained a representative, Bette Wimbish, on the City Council.

FREE SPIRITS

In their own unique way, they were St. Petersburg's celebrities — seen daily downtown, dedicatedly pursuing their unusual lives, and in one case, mysterious, silent anonymity. For the most part, their many friends and fans never knew their real names or from where they arrived.

One such character identified himself as Tennessee Slim, "St. Petersburg's smallest merchant." A former alcoholic from Chattanooga, Tennessee Slim ran a small fishing shop on First Avenue South but usually wasn't in it. He preferred pedaling around town on his balloon-tired bicycle, carrying his small companion dog. Tennessee Slim enjoyed being a town character, and saw little need to use his real name, James C. Beavers.

The kindest face to ever grace downtown was that of Elijah "I Got 'Em" Moore. A rangy, aged, black man in a top hat, he roamed through downtown on his daily bicycle rounds, chanting "I Got 'Em" as he sold perfectly roasted peanuts. "I came here in 1912 when this place was nothing but a woods," Moore told the *Times* in 1965 while making his downtown rounds on his 86th birthday.

Causing occasional downtown traffic jams in the 1960s was Esther Wright, the Bird Lady. Dedicated to caring for birds, the delicate former painter punctually rode from park to park on her tricycle, tossing seeds and scraps collected from restaurant dumpsters. Her daily mission, undertaken because "the birds would starve without me," disrupted homeward-bound traffic as hundreds of birds swooped down to greet her. But no motorist was callous enough to file a complaint.

As a free spirit, Franklin Burke was St. Petersburg's most peripatetic ambassador. He couldn't sit still to march music. Dressing up in homemade Uncle Sam, Abe Lincoln, or Indian Chief costumes, and strapping on roller skates, Burke couldn't resist joining, uninvited, any parade or patriotic event. During one Williams Park band concert, the director halted the music to yell, "Franklin, will you sit down? My musicians are watching you, not me."

His most ignominious performance occurred in Washington D.C. when he crashed newly elected President Carter's Inaugural Parade. Just as Burke reached the Presidential reviewing stand, a wheel spun off his $10 skates and he sprawled onto the pavement.

Never to be identified, perhaps, was the Blue Angel. A trimly attractive young woman with blonde, straight, ear-length hair, she wore all dark blue — always with a turtleneck collar. Patrons at the Open-air Post Office saw her daily. From there she would walk quietly, always alone, back to Central Avenue or toward Williams Park and disappear. Before she did, however, she sometimes "modeled" for startled onlookers. She would walk, head high, to a street corner, twirl slowly one way, then another, as though parading the latest Paris couture, then would regally stroll to the next corner and repeat the performance.

Of all St. Petersburg's free spirits, this elegant, mysterious woman-in-blue was perhaps the most intriguing. She was never heard to speak a word.

One young man, determined to learn her identity, gently blocked her path and kindly inquired, "Please — would you tell me who you are?"

The Blue Angel stared at him vacantly, seeming to ponder the question. In stony silence, she stepped around him. And, alas, into perpetual anonymity.

CHARACTERS ROAMED the city, showing up at any function that attracted a crowd and thus attention to them. Parades were their specialties, and although they never were included in the official lineup, they always wiggled their way in between floats or bands or clowns. One of the perpetual crowd-seekers was Tennessee Slim, whose trademark vehicle was a bicycle. His constant companion, a tiny dog, either rode with him in a two-wheel trailer or in a basket on the bike's handlebars. Slim ran a small fishing tackle shop on First Avenue South and called himself the city's smallest merchant. His bicycle signs refer to fellow Tennessean Doc Webb, the city's largest merchant.

THE NEW MUNICIPAL PIER BUILDING shortly after opening in 1973.

LUXURY HIGH-RISE APARTMENTS, or condominiums, began squeezing into the strip with a waterfront view between Beach Drive (*right*) and North Shore Drive (*left*) in the 1960s and 1970s. The city's first high-rise success was considered to be the 184-unit Carlton Towers on Third Street South between Fourth and Fifth avenues. Success of the high-rises near downtown has been attributed to their being within walking distance of recreation, shopping, and the work place. Their popularity also increased the value and prices of downtown real estate. Whereas in 1880 the 14-acre Vinoy Park Hotel tract sold for only $36, in 1988 the small 26-stool National Bar and Package Store on Central Avenue and Second Street sold for $1 a square foot.

MUSIC MAN

Shore Acres in the 1970s was the scene of a wondrous occasion that occurred in an equally unique residence: a circular one-story house with rooms leading off a balcony every 20 degrees or so that overlooked a sunken living room. The home belonged to Herb Melleney, managing director of the Festival of States.

Melleney loved marching bands. And in the 1970s there was no more celebrated band in the world than Largo's Band of Gold, winner of international awards over professional marching units from as distant as New Zealand.

One night each Spring Melleney delighted in bringing the Festival of States home with him, where the 200-plus-member Band of Gold lined up four deep around the balcony and struck up a plaster-pulsing rendition of Beethoven's Ninth Symphony. Wine glasses tottered on their stems. Hors d'oeuvres bounced on their trays. Lights snapped on up and down the neighborhood street. Had Beethoven not been deaf before composing his symphony, his hearing certainly would have suffered, at least temporarily, on one of those Spring nights as a guest of Melleney's.

The annual ear-splitting soiree was one of Melleney's favorite creations during the Festival. And he produced many, including the always sold-out Tournament of Champions, a massed band festival at Al Lang Stadium.

Prior to Melleney's era, the Festival had been little more than a tableau of pretty maidens set upon the banks of Round Lake, near north Fourth Street. In the official 1940 program, featured was a "Phosphorescent Fantasy," a ballet starring the four winds. Another early staging offered "Reflections in the Water," in which "charming misses in yards of pale organdy" were serenaded by "a clear voice singing of trees and skies and waters blue."

By 1958, the Suncoasters, a volunteer group of city business and professional leaders, rescued the Festival from drowning in Round Lake. Scrapping the tulle and organdy musicals, Melleney and the Suncoasters instituted a two-week, nonstop, dawn-to-midnight music spectacle that soon prompted tourists to schedule their Florida vacations to coincide with the Festival of States.

To produce such a show, starring scores of visiting and instate marching bands, was a mammoth undertaking. Every out-of-state band marched in two parades, provided a free Williams Park band concert, and competed in a variety of musical competitions, culminating in the Tournament, a contest of halftime-show pageantry.

There were plenty of headaches — from event coordination to ensuring the high school participants were safe and comfortable to keeping the massive Festival of States parade units moving. Parade crashers like Franklin Burke gave the Suncoasters fits. Burke always dressed up as Uncle Sam, donned his roller skates, and managed to haunt the parade from start to finish. The crowd loved his patriotism, but Burke's antics played havoc with the parade's lineup.

By Festival's end each year, Melleney's bloodshot eyes were underpinned by two huge bags.

To some, Herb Melleney was a gruff personality, but everyone agreed his perfectionistic staging of the annual Festival of States brought the civic celebration to its zenith.

THE ONE EVENT SELLING OUT year after year has been the Tournament of Champions, a weeknight musical competition held at Al Lang Stadium during the Festival of States celebration. The five-hour show features between 2,000 and 4,000 high school band musicians from around the country in a marching musical competition. The photo taken in 1976 shows the massed bands lined up to learn the judges' decision.

STRUTTING DOWN BAYSHORE DRIVE, the North Whitfield Pioneer Band from Dalton GA leads a Festival of States promenade in the 1970s that stepped off in front of the Vinoy Park Hotel and continued more than a mile before disbanding on Central Avenue west of Ninth Street. This was the hours-long daytime parade, usually held on Saturday. It came a few days after the musicians and floats participated in the nightime Illuminated Parade. High school bands in the annual Festival came by invitation only. For most of the youngsters, it was their first journey far from home. Most bands were invited two to three years before their appearance, giving them time for hometown fund-raising projects to pay for the trip.

THE NEW, ALL CONCRETE AL LANG STADIUM was ready for play in 1977. The ballpark has had a presence on the site since 1922, when a ballfield and grandstand were constructed and the facility named City Park. In 1947 the ballpark was renamed Al Lang Field and a new wooden grandstand built. It remained until the new stadium above was constructed at a cost of $3.5 million, with seating for 7,500. At center is the Bayfront Towers, a condominium built in 1975.

READY FOR ACTION in 1990 is the $110-million plus Florida Suncoast Dome, built on a 66-acre site between 10th and 16th Streets South and First and Fourth avenues. Without assurance the city would be awarded a Major League baseball franchise, St. Petersburg and Pinellas County organized the Pinellas Sport Authority in 1977 and proceeded with plans to build a domed stadium. The above site, which was the old St. Petersburg Gas Plant area, was chosen over sites in north St. Petersburg and in mid-county. Weighing 1,300 tons, the 8.5-acre translucent fiberglass dome, and the building, were built to withstand winds of 135 mph. The winning name for the structure in a citizens vote was Florida Suncoast Dome. Three years later the name was to be changed to ThunderDome.

SEATING CAPACITY FOR BASEBALL is 43,000, but seating varies with the type of event within the dome. Various configurations are possible so that football games will accommodate 37,400 people, soccer 33,670, basketball 32,950, and concerts 52,926. Height of the dome is 240 feet. Its diameter is 688 feet. The facility has 49 restrooms. Temperature inside is set at 72 degrees. After perpetual promotion and lobbying, St. Petersburg was granted a new Major League franchise. The team, named the Tampa Bay Devil Rays, will begin playing its first season in 1998.

TIMES AND ATTITUDES CHANGED greatly during St. Petersburg's 100-year history
and none proved more of a 180-degree switch than the residents opinion of the Gulf
beaches. In the 1920s and before, the beaches were viewed as a mosquito-plagued,
sand and salt stretch of waterfront to be avoided. The place was useless and
uncomfortable. By the post-World War II era, the same beaches were promoted as a
jewel among St. Petersburg's many assets. Metropolitan areas such as Tampa and
Orlando, competing for tourists, could not offer what St. Petersburg now pitched as a
sub-tropical paradise of sand and surf. Pass-a-Grille beach, pictured here, became one
of the most popular sunbathing and swimming sites along the state's west coast. In
this 1970s photo, the beach appears somewhat denuded of trees for years earlier it was
heavily landscaped with towering Australian pines. They were destroyed by storms,
some bringing high winds, others blowing in freezing temperatures.

FEW LANDMARKS REMAIN from 19th Century St. Petersburg. One is the Fountain of Youth, the artesian well given the city by one of its pioneers, E. H. Tomlinson. It is south of Al Lang Stadium just north of the Bayfront Center. For decades, tourists and residents filled their drinking jugs with the sulphur water, some even washing in it. "When I started coming here in 1952," an oldtimer told *Times'* columnist Dick Bothwell 10 years later, "I couldn't walk a block. Now I dance, swim, play ball." The Parks Department had to move the well's fountain a few yards in 1946 when an expanded Al Lang Field was built, but the city assured residents the Fountain of Youth was too symbolic and historic to ever be done away with. Yet in 1988, although it did not disturb the sunken spa, the city turned off the flow of water. Park officials explained that the Pinellas County Health Department required the water be cut off because it did not contain sufficient chlorine to be safe. The landmark structure remains, but not its curative waters.

St. Petersburg Chronology

1837 • William Bunce settles at Mullet Key.
1843 • First Pinellas Point white settler is fisherman Antonio Maximo Hernandez.
1845 • Florida becomes a state.
1848 • St. Petersburg hit directly by unnamed hurricane nicknamed "The Great Gale."
1857 • Abel Miranda arrives at Big Bayou area.
1859 • Bethell brothers set up fishing business at south end of Pinellas County.
1875 • John C. Williams makes initial visit to Point Pinellas.
1876 • Big Bayou Post Office established and named Pinellas.
1879 • Williams returns from Michigan to farm on Point Pinellas, fails, returns home.
1881 • Hamilton Disston buys 4,000 Point Pinellas acres at a price of 25-cents per acre.
1884 • Plat filed for Disston City.
1885 • Ward's School is started by R.E. Ward family at Big Bayou.
      • Dr. W. C. Van Bibber recommends health benefits of Point Pinellas to American Medical Society, declaring it "healthiest spot on earth."
1886 • First newspaper, the weekly *South Florida Home,* begins publication.
      • Newly remarried Williams returns to Florida and lives in Tampa's Hyde Park.
1887 • Peter Demens names settlement St. Petersburg after his Russian city.
      • Williams and Demens agree to run Demens' Orange Belt Railway into St. Petersburg.
      • Williams moves to Big Bayou.
      • St. Bartholomew Episcopal Church built.
1888 • First Orange Belt Railway train arrives.
      • Town plat recorded.
      • Williams builds Detroit Hotel.
      • City park (later renamed Williams Park) is platted.
      • Little Wooden School opens at Central Avenue and Fifth Street.
1889 • Pier built off First Avenue South into Tampa Bay for use by railroad and ships.
      • Demens departs Florida.
1890 • Williams builds home at Fourth Street and Fifth Avenue South.
      • First Williams Park bandshell constructed.
      • Paxton Hotel opens at Central Avenue and First Street.
1892 • Williams dies.
      • First town jail erected at Ninth Street and First Avenue South.
      • *West Hillsborough Times* moves to St. Petersburg.
      • St. Petersburg is incorporated as a city.
1893 • Williams Park fenced to keep out cattle.
      • "Graded" school built on present City Hall site.
1894 • Severe freeze hits all of Florida.
      • Claraden Hotel built at Central Avenue and First Street.
1895 • Financially strapped Orange Belt Railway operation leased to Henry Plant and renamed the Sanford & St. Petersburg Railway.
1896 • Second (Brantley's) pier, with bath pavilion and toboggan slide, built into bay at foot of Second Avenue North.
      • Washington Birthday celebrations begin (forerunner of Festival of States).
      • Hamilton Disston dies.
1897 • F. A. Davis builds electric generating plant on waterfront.
      • Major downtown streets resurfaced using shell from Mound Park.
1898 • *West Hillborough Times* newspaper is renamed *St. Petersburg Times.*
      • Fort De Soto constructed.

1899 • St. Petersburg Chamber of Commerce organizes.
 • Public phone system installed.
 • Steamer line operates between Tampa and St. Petersburg.
 • St. Petersburg Episcopal Church built at Fourth Street North and Second Avenue.
 • Henry Plant dies.
1900 • St. Petersburg population 1,575.
 • Fountain of Youth, an artesian well, opens on waterfront.
1901 • Formation of the Woman's Town Improvement Association.
1902 • Bell telephone line completed to Tampa.
 • St. Petersburg Chamber of Commerce reorganizes.
 • First state tourist society – Illinois – meets.
 • Sanford & St. Petersburg Railway merges with Atlantic Coast Line system.
1903 • Town of St. Petersburg granted a city charter by State Legislature.
 • First National Bank opens.
 • Brick used to pave major thoroughfares.
1905 • Trolley system opens New Year's Day.
 • First automobile, an Orient, driven to St. Petersburg by E. H. Tomlinson.
 • Disston City (now Gulfport) renamed Veteran City.
 • Seven city hotels provide 675 rooms for visitors.
 • Newly formed Board of Trade begins purchasing waterfront acreage to hold in trust for later purchase by city.
 • Royal Palm Theater begins showing moving pictures.
1906 • Brantley's pier replaced by Davis's "Electric Pier" (near site of today's Municpal Pier).
 • *St. Petersburg Independent* established as weekly newspaper.
 • Steamer traffic increases.
1907 • Routine overland trips from St. Petersburg to Tampa take three days.
 • Davis's enterprises (real estate, steamer lines, streetcars, power plant) fail and forced into receivership.
 • *St. Petersburg Independent* becomes afternoon daily and name is changed to the *Evening Independent*.
1908 • Real estate salesman Noel Mitchell places first street benches in front of his Fourth Street and Central Avenue office.
 • *Evening Independent* purchased by Lew Brown.
1909 • Board of Trade reorganizes under name of Chamber of Commerce.
1910 • Population 4,127.
 • Samaritan Emergency Hospital opens.
 • Veteran City renames itself Gulfport.
 • Lew Brown offers free copies of *Evening Independent* newspaper any day the sun fails to shine.
 • Waterfront Park officially becomes city-owned for public use.
1911 • Poinsettia Hotel opens.
 • Pinellas County is created out of part of Hillsborough County (May 23).
 • Domed St. Petersburg High School is built at Second Avenue and Fifth Street North.
 • C. Perry Snell and J. C. Hamlett launch North Shore development.
 • City purchases Round Lake for $600.
 • Davis's "Electric Pier" demolished.
 • Charles Roser buys 30 acres along Booker Creek.

1912 • First recorded flight in St. Petersburg by L. W. Bonney.
    • Federal funding approved for deep-water harbor at Bayboro, project stymied by public opposition.
1913 • La Plaza Theater opens.
    • Special train brings some 200 Winter visitors from Ohio and Indiana.
    • Augusta Memorial Hospital built on former Indian shell mound.
    • Spa Pool bathhouse opens at North Mole beach.
    • New recreation/freight pier begun at Second Avenue North.
    • Public approves Bayboro Harbor project.
1914 • World's first commercial airline established with Tony Jannus's scheduled airboat flights between St. Petersburg and Tampa.
    • St. Louis Browns begin Spring training at Coffee Pot Bayou diamond.
    • Willson-Chase opens five-story department store.
    • Gas plant under construction.
    • Southland Seminary opens on Coffee Pot Bayou.
    • Sixty-room addition made to Detroit Hotel.
1915 • Seaboard Air Line railroad purchases Tampa & Gulf Coast Railroad.
    • New ACL depot opens between Second and Third streets at First Avenue South.
    • Carnegie-funded Mirror Lake library opens.
    • Philadelphia Phillies begin Spring training (1915-1918) in city.
    • Construction starts on St. Petersburg Country Club on First Avenue North.
1916 • Jannus dies in World War I air crash.
    • St. Petersburg Country Club is city's first golf course (later known as Jungle Club).
    • Augusta Memorial Hospital renamed City Hospital.
    • St. Petersburg Lawn Bowling Club founded.
    • Open-air Post Office construction begins.
1917 • St. Petersburg Yacht Club opens.
    • City stages first Festival of States celebration.
    • Open-air Post Office dedicated.
1918 • Masons buy Southland Seminary on Coffee Pot Bayou for use as Masonic home.
    • World War I armistice, war claims 16 soldiers from St. Petersburg.
1919 • McAdoo Bridge to beaches opens to traffic.
    • Hotel Alexander (75 rooms) built on Central Avenue between Fifth and Sixth streets.
    • Land around Crescent Lake purchased.
    • New St. Petersburg High School built (later to be Mirror Lake Junior High).
    • Pheil Theater built on Central Avenue.
1920 • Population 14,237.
    • St. Petersburg Historical Society chartered.
    • C. Perry Snell opens nine-hole private Coffee Pot Golf Course.
1921 • Hurricane strikes, causing 10-foot tides.
    • Plans for a "Million-Dollar Pier" introduced.
    • *St. Petersburg Times* moves to Fifth Street and First Avenue South corner.
1922 • Jack Taylor buys 600 acres of raw land for Pasadena area development.
    • Historic Museum opens on Municipal Pier.
    • Boston Braves start Spring training (1922-1927) in city.
    • St. Petersburg Yacht Club enlarged.
    • Waterfront park ballfield and grandstand built.
    • Ponce de Leon Hotel built at Central Avenue and Beach Drive.

1923 • First shuffleboard courts marked out at Mirror Lake.
• Bayboro Harbor facility completed.
• City Hospital renamed Mound Park Hospital.
• Suwannee Hotel opens at First Avenue and Fifth Street North.
1924 • Gandy Bridge opens ($3 million), reducing trip between St. Petersburg and Tampa from 43 miles to 19 miles.
• Bayboro Power Plant built at Third Street South and 13th Avenue.
• Mason Hotel opens.
• Pheil Hotel opens.
• Coliseum opens (cost $250,000).
• Soreno Hotel opens.
• Lakewood Estates under development.
• Hall Building built at southeast corner of Central Avenue and Fourth Street.
1925 • Greatest expansion of city land – voters add 38.47 acres to city.
• Jungle Country Club (later Admiral Farragut site) built for $680,000.
• Doc Webb opens "cut-rate" drug store.
• New York Yankees begin Spring training (1925-1961) at Crescent Lake Field.
• Florida Power Corp. headquarters built at First Avenue and Fifth Street South.
• St. Petersburg Kennel Club opens.
• Vinoy Park Hotel ($3-million) opens.
• Real estate boom starts souring.
1926 • YMCA opens ($500,000).
• Florida Theater opens (six stories, 2,300 seats).
• Rolyat Hotel opens.
• Million-Dollar Pier opens.
• New St. Petersburg High School built on Fifth Avenue North.
• Bee Line Ferry opens.
• Mason Hotel renamed the Princess Martha.
• Snell Isle Garden Apartments completed.
• Port of St. Petersburg (Bayboro Harbor) established off 7th Avenue South.
1927 • WSUN radio begins broadcasts from Municipal Pier.
• St. Petersburg Junior College created.
• Salvation Army Citadel completed at Third Street South.
• Rolyat Hotel fails.
• Opening of Gibbs High School.
• U.S. Coast Guard Base established at Bayboro Harbor.
1928 • Sky Harbor Airport begins operation on Weedon Island.
• Sunset Golf and Country Clubhouse built.
• Don Ce-Sar opens.
1929 • Stock market crashes.
• Downtown waterfront airfield named Albert Whitted Field in honor of local aviator killed in Pensacola crash.
• Tramor Cafeteria built.
• Goodyear blimps start flying from Albert Whitted Air Field.
• Waterfront Park encompasses 90 acres, dredging and filling continues to enlarge area.
• Snell Building at Central Avenue and Fourth Street completed ($750,000).
1930 • Population 40,425.
• Scrip used to pay many workers.
• St. Petersburg banks fail.
• Sunbathing Solarium built along Municipal Pier.

1931	• Kids & Kubs Three-Quarter Century Softball Club incorporated.
	• National Shuffleboard Association organized at Mirror Lake.
1932	• Florida Military Academy moves into Rolyat Hotel.
1933	• Bay Pines Veterans Hospital opens.
	• Sun Haven (film) Studios in production on Weedon Island.
	• Charter issued for First Federal Savings & Loan Association.
1934	• National Airlines begins with four-passenger plane flight from Albert Whitted airport to Daytona Beach.
	• Davis Causeway (later renamed Courtney Campbell) opens.
	• Woman's Town Improvement Association disbanded.
1935	• High winds blow down twin Moorish towers on Coliseum.
1936	• City converts public transit from streetcars to buses.
1937	• Wing added to Mound Park Hospital.
1938	• St. Louis Cardinals (1938-42, 1946 to present) begin St. Petersburg Spring training.
	• Pinellas County buys Mullet Key from U.S. Government.
1939	• City Hall built and dedicated.
	• Treasure Island Causeway finished.
1940	• Population 60,812.
	• WTSP radio goes on air.
	• Jordan Park housing development opens.
1941	• Pinellas County Airport constructed.
1942	• City serves as military basic training site.
	• Military "Tent City" built at west end of Fifth Avenue North on Boca Ciega Bay.
	• Don Ce Sar Hotel sold to government for use as military convalescent center.
1944	• Gandy Bridge and Davis Causeway cease tolls.
1945	• Admiral Farragut Academy takes over Jungle Country Club Hotel.
	• Alsonett Hotel chain buys Vinoy Park Hotel for $700,000.
1947	• Al Lang Field dedicated.
1948	• Pinellas County buys Fort De Soto from U.S. Government.
	• Alsonett Hotel chain buys Sunset Golf and Country Club.
	• Maas Brothers Department store opens.
1949	• Final streetcar run.
1950	• Population 96,738.
	• Dredge and fill of Boca Ciega Bay begins.
1951	• Tyrone Garden Shopping Center opens.
	• Addition built to Mirror Lake Library.
	• Trolley tracks removed from city streets.
	• Florida Military Academy based at Rolyat Hotel closes down.
	• New jail constructed at 1300 First Avenue North.
1952	• Central Plaza Shopping Center built in Goose Pond area.
1953	• WSUN-TV goes on the air in St. Petersburg.
	• Boca Ciega High School opens.
1954	• Sunshine Skyway bridge opens, $1.75 toll.
	• Former Rolyat Hotel becomes Stetson College of Law.
	• Bee Line Ferry makes final trip.
	• Northeast High School opens.
1957	• La Plaza Theater demolished.
	• Kenneth City created by Sidney Colen.
	• New main Post Office building opens at First Avenue North and 31st Street.

1958 • Skyway bridge toll reduced to $1.
     • WEDU educational television goes on air.
     • Suncoasters organized.
1959 • Dixie Hollins High School opens.
1960 • Population 181,298.
     • Florida Presbyterian College holds first classes at Bayboro Harbor Maritime Base.
     • Howard Frankland Bridge opens.
1961 • Green benches painted over with pastel colors and many removed.
     • Bayway construction begins to link 54th Avenue South to St. Petersburg Beach.
     • Tierra Verde development gets under way.
     • Solarium along Municipal Pier demolished.
1962 • Pastel benches repainted green.
     • Spa Pool razed.
     • New York Mets begin Spring training (1962-1987) in St. Petersburg.
     • *St. Petersburg Times* purchases *Evening Independent*.
     • *Evening Independent* building is demolished.
1963 • Florida Presbyterian College moves to present-day Eckerd College site.
     • Last ACL passenger train departs downtown depot.
     • Nine-hundred-acre Fort De Soto Park dedicated.
1964 • New library built on Ninth Avenue North.
1965 • *HMS Bounty* replica arrives to become waterfront attraction.
     • Museum of Fine Arts opens.
     • Bayfront Center opens.
1966 • Hurricane Alma sideswipes city with 90 mph winds.
     • Black activists tear down mural in City Hall.
     • Lakewood High School opens.
     • Skyway tolls reduced to 50 cents.
     • Willson-Chase department store files bankruptcy.
1967 • Florida Theater demolished.
     • Million-Dollar Pier demolished.
     • Federal Building opens on First Avenue South.
     • West Coast Inn razed.
1968 • Royal Palm and Tropic hotels razed for expansion of *St. Petersburg Times*.
     • Garbage workers strike.
     • Racial unrest hits city.
     • Two thousand teachers strike.
1969 • WTOG-TV begins broadcasting.
     • South side of Open-air Post Office enclosed.
     • *Evening Independent* records record 765 days of consecutive sunshine in city.
     • Lutheran Apartments, Presbyterian Towers, John Knox Apartments built.
1970 • Population 216,232.
     • Bette Wimbish elected first black on City Council.
     • Oil spill stains Tampa Bay and beaches.
1971 • Twin span of Sunshine Skyway opens.
     • Florida Presbyterian College renamed for benefactor Jack Eckerd.
     • Pinellas County schools desegregated.
     • Downtown Hilton Hotel opens.
1972 • Hurricane Agnes floods Shore Acres.
     • Florida Power Corp. moves into new 34th Street South headquarters.

1973 • New, pyramidal-shaped Municipal Pier building opens.
    • St. Petersburg voted an "All-American City" by National Municipal League.
1974 • Webb's City sold.
    • Museum of Fine Arts adds theater.
    • Vinoy Park Hotel closes.
1975 • Christian Science Monitor names St. Petersburg one of the 10 "most livable cities."
    • Al Lang Field wooden grandstand razed for rebuilding.
    • Bayfront Towers opens.
1976 • Bayboro Power Plant smokestacks demolished.
1977 • Demens' Landing, formerly the nine-acre South Mole, dedicated.
    • Bicentennial waterfront fountain erected in Straub Park.
    • City buys Edgewater Beach Motel east of the Vinoy Park Hotel.
    • New $3.5 million Al Lang Stadium opens.
1978 • Hall Building razed.
    • I-275 opens.
    • Plaza office and shopping complex opens on Second Avenue North.
    • Ground broken for the University of South Florida's St. Petersburg campus.
1979 • Webb's City closes.
1980 • Sunshine Skyway, rammed by freighter, incurs severe damage to both spans.
1982 • Jannus Landing, a square block of rehabbed historic buildings, opens.
    • Dali Museum built.
1985 • Poynter Institute begins operations.
1986 • *HMS Bounty* sails out of town.
    • *St. Petersburg Times* ceases publication of *Evening Independent*
1987 • New Sunshine Skyway ($224-million) opens.
    • Great Explorations Museum dedicated.
    • Center Theater (formerly Alcazar and Roxy) at Central Avenue and Ninth Street razed.
1988 • Renovated Bayfront Center opens.
    • Pinellas County Health Department turns off Fountain of Youth waters.
1989 • City purchases Coliseum.
1990 • Florida Suncoast Dome finished.
1991 • Maas Brothers department store closes.
1992 • Soreno Hotel razed.
    • Renovated Vinoy Park Hotel opens to guests as Renaissance Vinoy Resort.
    • Florida Lightning begins National Hockey League play.
1993 • Florida Suncoast Dome renamed ThunderDome.
1995 • Florida International Museum opens in former Maas Brothers department store.
    • City granted Major League baseball team franchise with team named Tampa Bay Devil Rays to begin scheduled play in 1998.

Origin of St. Petersburg Place Names

Abercrombie Park — Honors Dr. John B. Abercrombie, an early practitioner who arrived in 1883 from Natchez MS.

Al Lang Field and Stadium — Named to honor the early mayor, avid baseball fan, and promoter of Major League Spring training in St. Petersburg.

Albert Whitted Airport — Honors World War I and commercial pilot who was killed in his plane near Pensacola.

Allendale — Upscale development named for builder Cade Allen.

Bartlett Park — Named for early civic leader and educator A. F. Barlett.

Binninger Center for Performing Arts (at Eckerd College) — Honors Fort Lauderdale minister Clem Binninger, who funded the center.

Blanton Elementary School — R. S. Blanton, Pinellas County superintendent of schools from 1921 to 1928.

Boca Ciega — Spanish for "blind mouth," referring to the bay's configuration.

Boyd Hill Nature Center — Named for former director of St. Petersburg Parks and Recreation Department.

Bunce's Pass — William Bunce was a fisherman and an early settler of Mullet Key.

Courtney Campbell Causeway — Named for State Road Board member.

Cramer Federal Building — Named for former Florida Congressman Bill Cramer.

Crisp Park — Named for developers Frank and Robert Crisp.

Demens' Landing — Named for Peter Demens, a Russian emigrant and co-founder of St. Petersburg.

Disston (school and community) — Named for early developer Hamilton Disston.

Dixie Hollins High School — Honors early Pinellas County school superintendent who served from 1912 to 1920.

Eckerd College — Named after drugstore magnate and college benefactor James Eckerd.

Edward White Hospital — Named for an astronaut killed in a fire aboard Apollo I in 1967.

Flora Wylie Park — Honors the 1928 founder of St. Petersburg Garden Club.

Frank Pierce Community Center — Named to honor leading black educator and civic activist.

Frenchman's Creek — Believed to be named for pioneer "Frenchman" John Lavique.

Gandy Bridge — Named after bridge builder George Gandy.

Gibbs High School — Salutes Jonathan Gibbs, a Florida Secretary of State during Reconstruction days who founded Florida A & M University.

Haines Road — Honors G. B. Haines, an area advocate of advanced road building techniques.

Howard Frankland Bridge — Tampa businessman and civic leader.

Huggins-Stengel Field — Miller Huggins and Casey Stengel, New York Yankees managers.

Jack Puryear Park — Honors longtime director of the St. Petersburg Parks and Recreation Department.

Jamestown — Fomerly Methodist Town and renamed in honor of the Rev. Chester James, area black activitist in the 1970s.

Jannus Landing — Recognizes Tony Jannus, pioneer aviator who established first air service between St. Petersburg and neighboring cities.

Joe's Creek — Thought to be named for Joe Silva, an early turtler, who lived about a mile from the creek.

John's Pass — Reputedly named for John Levique, an early settler, fisherman, and turtler who first discovered that a storm had created the new pass.

Jordan Park — Named for black civic leader Elder Jordan Sr.

Lake Maggiore — Named in 1884 on the Disston City plat after famous Italian lake, Maggiore-Lago, it was popularly referred to as Salt Lake. In the 1920s, Lakewood subdivision developer Charles Hall restored the name Lake Maggiore on his plat.

Lassing Park — Honors Robert B. Lassing, property owner on St. Petersburg's south side and early president of the St. Petersburg Yacht Club.

Lawson Stadium — Named for Bentley Lawson, first principal of Dixie Hollins High School.

Lealman (school and community) — W. M. Lealman, area founder and developer.

Lynch Elementary School — Recognizes Capt. George M. Lynch, early Pinellas County school superintendent from 1929 to 1935.

Mahaffey Theater — Honors St. Petersburg philanthropists Thomas and Jane Mahaffey.

Maximo Point — Homesite of early settler Antonio Maximo Hernandez.

Nina Harris School — Named for area educator and young people's advocate.

Norwood Elementary School — Named for Arthur Norwood, early Disston City teacher who became successful businessman and mayor of St. Petersburg.

Papy's Bayou — Believed named after Antonio Papy, a fisherman and Count Odet Philippe's son-in-law, who settled on Weedon Island.

Perkins Elementary School — Named for prominent educator George W. Perkins.

Pinellas — From the Spanish for "Point of Pines."

Poynter Institute — Named for *St. Petersburg Times* owner Nelson Poynter.

Roberts Community Center — Dedicated to musician Robert W. Roberts by his widow.

Roser Park — Charles Roser, developer of area, original owner of the National Biscuit Co. (later Nabisco), and creator of the Fig Newton cookie.

Rutland Building — Formerly Snell Building, named for and by Hubert Rutland, banker, civic leader, and merchant.

Sexton Stadium — Named for first principal of Northeast High School, John Sexton.

Sheffield Lake — Named for pioneer Sheffield family, who settled the area around 49th Street and 22nd Avenue North.

Snell Isle — Development named after North Shore developer C. Perry Snell.

Stewart Field — Honors Fred K. Stewart, principal of St. Petersburg High School from 1947 to 1948.

Straub Park — Named for William Lincoln Straub, former owner and editor of the *St. Petersburg Times* who campaigned for public use of the city's waterfront.

Tierra Verde — Spanish for green land.

Tomlinson Adult Education Center — Named for St. Petersburg philanthropist Edwin H. Tomlinson, builder of the city's first manual training building, and the Fountain of Youth.

Vinoy Park Hotel — Named for builder Aymer Vinoy Laughner, member of a wealthy Pennsylvania oil family.

Walter Fuller Community Center — Honors the colorful boom-time developer and author of *St. Petersburg and its People.*

Weedon Island — Actually a peninsula, it is named for Dr. Leslie W. Weedon who settled it in 1898. Rich Indian and Spanish archaeological site.

Williams Park — First park in city, on lands donated by pioneer John C. Williams.

Index